HEARTBEATS

THE LIGHT-HEARTED MEMOIRS OF A PIONEER HEART SURGEON CONSTANTINE J. "DINO" TATOOLES, MD

James E. Tatooles

Illustrations by Thomas C. Katsulis

THE LIGHT-HEARTED MEMOIRS OF A PIONEER HEART SURGEON

Remembrances of Dr. Constantine J. "Dino" Tatooles, MS Physiology, FACS, FACC, ICUC, Member of American College of Thoracic Surgeons, Association of Thoracic Surgeons, International Society of Cardiac Surgeons, Head of Andrew G. Morrow Society 23 years, Senior Registrar, Hospital for Sick Children, Great Ormond Street, London, Surgical Resident, University of Chicago Hospital, Chairman and Professor of Surgery at University of Illinois Hospital, Cook County Hospital, and West Side Veterans Administration Hospital, Chief Cardiac Surgery at St. Francis Hospital, Evanston, Illinois, Staff Chief Cardiac Surgery St. Mary's Hospital, Chicago, Chairman Cardiovascular Surgery, Mt. Sinai, Chicago, Member Monte Carlo Cardiac Institute, Monaco.

Published by Open Books

Copyright © 2014 by James E. Tatooles

Cover and illustrations Copyright © 2014 by Thomas C. Katsulis

ISBN: 0692271325
ISBN-13: 978-0692271322

DEDICATION

To our mother, Angela J. Tatooles
Widowed too soon, as a single parent she eschewed
personal pursuits and instead dedicated her life to
raising, educating and providing for the well being
of her two sons.

.

OUR DAD'S SAGE ADVICE

- Get the most education possible, never stop reading or learning.
- Your job is to make the next generation better than yours.
- Be the best in whatever you do. Even if you are a bum, be the best bum.
- Don't forget your roots. Remember where you came from and be humble.
- A good deed is something to be accomplished without acknowledgement or fanfare.
- Self-Praise Stinks!
- Be a Cubs fan and a Bears fan...and vote Republican.
- Never go into the restaurant business, you will have to be on your feet all day*.

*While still operating late one afternoon Dino started laughing out loud to himself. The scrub team became concerned and asked him if anything was the matter? He said "I just remembered my dad's advice to not go into the restaurant business because I would be on my feet all day. I've been here bent over this table since 7:00 a.m. and couldn't even stop for a cup of coffee."

CONTENTS

FOREWORD

I have known Dr. C. J. "Dino" Tatooles since he was a surgical resident and consider him a good friend. Dino is one of those people who can be counted on to get any job done efficiently and, if possible, lightheartedly. This book is no exception. I thoroughly enjoyed reading about his fascinating adventures in cardiothoracic surgery. Dino got his start a little after me, but we both watched heart surgery evolve throughout the last half of the twentieth century—the most exciting times in the history of the specialty.

I met Dino in1967, when he came to Houston to visit Mike DeBakey and me on a "Coller Clinical Tour." Dr. Frederick Coller, an academic surgeon at the University of Michigan, had endowed a national "tour" that each year allowed two outstanding surgical residents to spend a month visiting a number of cardiovascular surgeons of their choosing. Mike and I were among a few Dino chose to visit, all of whom were pioneers in the field. The others were Gordon Danielson, Walt Lillehei, Al Merendino, Norman Shumway, and Al Starr. Dino would soon join us in the ranks of the pioneers, building his own career of "firsts."

When Dino visited me, my team and I were doing ten to fifteen heart surgeries in a day, and the specialty of heart surgery was still young. I like to think that I inspired him in some way to pursue lofty goals. I did encourage him to spend some time training abroad as I had done, and I was pleased to learn that he took my advice.

Reading *Heartbeats* reawakened my personal memories, including one of my most vivid remembrances of Dino. During the early days of heart transplantation, donors had to be physically transported to the facility where the transplant operation was to be performed, as no method was available to keep a donor heart viable outside the body for any length of time. I happened to learn that a donor heart was available in Chicago that would be a good size match for a baby who needed a heart transplant in Houston. Of course, I knew Dino was in Chicago, as he had just recently been to visit me, so I called him and asked him to bring the baby to me. Even though I didn't know him well at that time, I knew he would be up for any challenge, and I was right.

As the title attests, *Heartbeats* truly is a lighthearted account of an interesting man and an incredible career. I believe that the book will be enjoyable for anyone who likes good stories. The lively, conversational style is characterized by Dino's wit and humor. Instead of reading it straight through, one can open the book to any chapter and gain insights about the history of an amazing surgical specialty and about how a great career developed.

Dino begins his story by describing the importance of his grandmother (Yia Yia Olga) in developing his desire to become a physician. I am certain that his Yia Yia would be extremely proud of her legacy.

Denton A. Cooley, MD
President Emeritus
Texas Heart Institute, Houston, Texas

PROLOGUE

The innovative doctors who pioneered in heart surgery were like Christopher Columbus exploring in uncharted waters on a flat world. This book touches on a divergent lighter side of that journey as experienced and related to me by my brother, Constantine J. "Dino" Tatooles, MD, MS, FACS, AATS, ACA, AHA, AMA, ATS, AAS, CHA, CMS, CCS, ISMS, ITS, IMC, NYAS, RSM, STS, WJC, ACC, ACCP, ACS, ACC, FFYS, etc., etc., etc., and more importantly, my best friend!

Our idyllic childhood was interrupted when our dad died. A strong willed single parent, Mother then devoted her life to her children. Education was primary to our upbringing; I became an engineer and Dino became the gratifying "My son the Doctor". He could not have chosen a better time to be trained for his profession. During his surgical residency Dino received the prestigious "Coller Clinical Tour Fellowship". As a fellow, he met, learned from, worked with, and became a personal friend of many of the pioneers of heart and vascular surgery. It was a unique period in the advancement of modern medicine.

The heart became the focal point of diversified research. Since the days of the ancient Egyptian physicians, the heart had been a sacred and untouchable organ. Even in the nineteenth century that view was widely held. In 1883, the German Professor Dr. Albert Theodor Billroth, founder of modern abdominal surgery, passionately stated: "A surgeon who dares to suture a heart deserves to lose the esteem of his medical brethren."

Yet just eight years later, in 1891, Dr. H.C. Dalton sutured a pericardium (Heart Sac) in St Louis. In 1893, Dr. Daniel Hale Williams did the same at Providence Hospital on the south side of Chicago. In 1897, Dr. Ludwig Rehn was the first to suture the myocardium (Heart Muscle) in Frankfort, Germany. Instead of losing esteem, the doctors are heralded in medical history for their achievements.

After my brother added an MD to his name and became a noted surgeon, he was fair game for interrogation. Time or locale didn't matter; when out socially, invariably the queries would begin: "Doc, have you got a moment?" Then the questions started: "Is it better to have a by-pass or are stents just as good?" "I had a by-pass a month ago, when can I resume sex?" Someone once actually asked him, "If I continue to pound hard on my chest will that hurt my heart?" Dino honestly can't remember his answer.

"Most hearts are located slightly left of center in the chest, but some can be central and others located on the right side. Some are big, others small. A baby's heart is the size of a walnut, and many are deformed. Like faces, each heart has its own unique appearance." I had heard that explanation related to others many times when my brother Dino would phase into his Professorial mode. "Except for identical twins, people are distinctive in appearance; internally as well as externally! There is no such thing as a typical heart."

He often stated, "A stereotype heart attack is another myth. Sharp chest pains, an aching left arm, difficulty in breathing, dull stomach aches all might precede a heart attack—or not. False positives could be indigestion, overtaxed muscles, coronary artery spasms or a myriad of other episodes." Could it just be heartburn or a heart attack? Dino discussed this with patient after patient, never dreaming that someday he would prove the point with his own heart attack.

Each year in the United States there are more than one

million coronary revascularizations involving either angioplasty or by-pass procedures, according to a study in the *Journal of the American Medical Association*. The number has been steadily growing for more than fifty years. Many more are candidates, known or unknown, waiting to be treated. My brother, the heart surgeon, became another one of the statistics.

"It couldn't be possible. I thought I had the flu. Then I saw the EKG, Jim. I'd *had* a heart attack!" No warning, no pain, not a "typical" heart attack. Thankfully, he had a successful resolution.

Dino explained, "I woke up preparing for a busy day. It started at Saint Francis Hospital in Evanston, Illinois with the first of two by-pass cases at 8:00 a.m. By 4:00 p.m. I had finished the second case and then drove to Holy Cross (an hour away in south Chicago) for another scheduled operation. Nothing new, I've been chasing from hospital to hospital for at least forty years.

"We cleared a blocked carotid artery; a routine procedure. Everything went smoothly until I backed away from the table; after closing is when it hit me. I became light headed and saw that my scrub suit was drenched."

Dino, acting very uncharacteristically, sought assistance. "I asked the nurses to help me get to the recovery room; I had to lie down." 'Doctor,' she said, 'there has been a rash of Flu going around, seems like you caught something.' Maybe, I said, but my instincts feared something was strangely amiss. I asked to be hooked up for an EKG and had my blood drawn. The EKG was off the chart, the blood work too early to indicate a problem. I asked that the EKG be faxed to Tony at Christ Hospital."

Tony, Dino's son and my eldest nephew, is also a cardiovascular surgeon. He operates in a group practice at nearby Christ Community Hospital, about ten minutes away from Holy Cross. It seemed that the fax was just sent when Dr. Patrick Pappas, Tony's partner, appeared in the recovery room. "I've come to get you Dino; we're going over to Christ." Dino's offer to drive was rejected.

Dino monitored the Heart Unit staff at work. "I watched the scope as they were probing me with the catheter; both my main right and main left arteries were blocked. That's when Pat told me that Tony was in Minnesota giving a talk." Pat asked, 'What do you want us to do, Doctor?' I told him to operate. 'I know,' he said, 'the operating room is already prepared for us.' Twelve hours after he had initially stood next to an operating table, Dino was on one.

Tony, back from Minneapolis, joined us in the family waiting room. After an interminable waiting period, the phone in the room finally rang. Pat told Tony, "Everything went well; he is off the pump and heading to the ICU, a Quintuplet by-pass, no less." Dino personalized his long career in heart surgery by experiencing the same lifesaving procedure he routinely used to save the lives of others.

GENES I—Yia Yia

Mankind throughout the world has always been cared for by local "healers" when trained medical help was not available. Such was the case with our "Yia Yia" Olga (grandmother), who learned the skills necessary to administer to other's needs as a young girl in her native village of Kastri, Greece.

"It hurts, it really, really hurts!" sobbed Dino's little friend Tommy, just hit in the arm with a baseball bat. The two eight-year-old friends were playing in River Park, where they had been specifically told not to go. Coincidentally, both of their mothers had had things to do that sunny summer afternoon and had instructed the boys to stay nearby until they returned; and not to go to the park! Now what? "I know, let's go back to my house," said Dino in a suddenly inspired voice. "My grandma will know what to do. I've seen her help lots of injured people." Yia Yia, who lived with them, was apparently the answer.

Yia Yia consoled the little tike while examining his arm. It was easy to see that it was broken. Knowing what to do, she asked the boys to go out to the pear tree in the back yard. Tommy was told to hold tightly onto the tree with his good arm. Yia Yia grasped the broken limb, aligned the arm and gave it a sudden tug. Tommy screamed, and then looked relieved as the arm once again looked as it should. Back inside the house, she had Tommy sit on a chair in the kitchen. There she wrapped the arm with triangular pieces of white cotton cloth. They were saturated with clear Ouzo, a Greek liqueur mixed with ground-up pieces of the incense that Yia Yia used to cense the house when she blessed it. She gently patted the binding, squeezed out the excess liquid and formed a tight sleeve around the broken bone site. The white sleeve started to dry. As it hardened, Yia Yia placed Tommy's arm in a sling and asked Dino to walk him home to rest. Dino did so, secure in knowing that he had taken care of his friend's injury.

When the mothers returned, all thoughts of punishment for disobeying vanished as they concentrated on Tommy's plight. He was taken to the emergency room at Swedish Covenant, the nearby hospital. X-rays confirmed that Tommy's right humerus was indeed broken; they also confirmed that the bone had been set perfectly! The doctors only had to replace the ouzo-scented sleeve with a conventional plaster cast and Tommy was then sent home.

Underneath the aforementioned pear tree in the back yard was Yia Yia's personal garden. Aside from the usual onions, carrots, tomatoes, etc., the back rows along the garage wall contained her unusual collection of herbs, flowers and other unknowns plants used to make plasters or brew teas. They were harvested, laid out to dry, and then ground up and placed in little jars down in her special basement storage area. (I often conjectured that some of the flowers looked suspiciously like red poppies.) As relatives and friends stopped by and related their ills, Yia Yia would brew up a pot or stir up a smelly plaster and administer her medicine. Her cures must have worked because people kept coming back for more help.

Grandma was a wise, strong-willed lady, sure of herself and fiercely independent. A case in point: some years later, while walking to church, she was struck by a car. Fortunately, the car just tapped her but still sent her sprawling to the pavement. Another trip to the Swedish Covenant X-ray department; this time it was a hairline fracture of the pelvis. A body cast was placed around her mid-section and she was sent to a recovery room. When Mom went to visit Yia Yia the next day she was asked to bring some fruit and a small paring knife. After supper, Yia Yia enjoyed her new assortment of fruit for dessert.

Early the next morning the hospital called and asked that someone come immediately. Dad had already gone to work so Mom, apprehensively, made the trip alone. She was told that during the night Yia Yia had used the small paring knife *to cut off the body cast*. Grandma explained to Mom and to the doctors that if the body cast had not been removed she would never walk again. After much wrangling and negotiating it was agreed that the cast would be replaced with a soft flexible bundled cloth and tape version. Yia Yia assured everyone that she would take on the responsibility of keeping still as required. When the soft cast was finally removed, Yia Yia had little trouble walking.

It is apparent that the genes were passed on to Dino from his grandmother. He saw her taking care of people as he grew up and wanted to do the same. Needless to say, he also took on her traits of a strong will, confidence and independence.

THE PARKING LOT

The best made plans of mice and men...

The passenger's seat suddenly felt warm. Water darkened the car floor mat; the young couple had waited too long. The woman's water had broken and there was no time to waste. Even at excessive speed, racing down Edens Expressway, they couldn't reach Chicago Passavant Hospital in time. Fortunately, the husband remembered that by turning east at Foster Avenue he could make it to Swedish Covenant Hospital in just a few more minutes. Racing into the hospital emergency room parking lot, his horn honking, he didn't even have time to get out of the car. The baby could wait no longer and started to stick its head out for a look at the world. The panicked husband had to stay with his wife, trying to console her.

New Interns and resident doctors have historically been underpaid. As others had done before him to supplement income, Dino worked weekends as an extern at the Swedish Covenant Hospital emergency department. He was on duty that Saturday evening when a blaring horn in the parking lot alerted him to run to the noisy car in the driveway. Acting on instinct, he delivered the baby in the front seat of the car. He finished by placing the newborn, umbilical cord still attached, into the loving arms of the anxious passenger. Nurses and other personnel quickly took over and brought the newborn child into the maternity ward of the hospital. The parents could not have been happier.

Dino, of course, also was exhilarated. He couldn't wait to talk about what had taken place in the parking lot of the hospital. But he held off calling his mother, Angela, until he knew she'd be awake. First thing in the morning he phoned and told her about his experience delivering a baby in the front seat of a car in the Swedish Covenant Emergency parking lot.

The proud mother listened attentively, reflecting that Dino had been born in the same hospital. "That was wonderful," she remarked wistfully. Then, after a moment of silence, she asked, "Was there a doctor there?" Dino was not a doctor; he was still just her baby.

GENES II—Uncle George, MD

They might have traveled by horseback, by carriage, or eventually in the family sedan. They came when called, brought hope to the sick and stayed as long as needed. Most doctors, apart from being dedicated to their oath, had two things in common: they made house calls and they all carried a little black bag.

Uncle George, not to be outdone, made some of his visits by parachute. Not for typical house calls, of course; this particular service lasted three years. Extremely Hazardous Duty, little likelihood of survival; one hundred and fifty dedicated, brave men stepped forward, and Captain George C. Markoutsas, MD was soon parachuting into German occupied Greece during the Second World War with the elite, all volunteer OSS Commando group, commonly known as the "Greek Battalion". A medical supply chute dropped nearby temporarily replaced his little black bag.

The *Office of Strategic Services*, Robert Donovan's war effort brain child, was the forerunner of today's CIA. Under cover ethnically related units were formed to rendezvous with and assist partisans with behind the lines resistance efforts. There were German, French and Italian Battalions in addition to the Greeks. Many of the other groups working behind enemy lines were killed or captured in the line of duty. The Greek Battalion fortunately lost only two souls and had just a few wounded men.

After completing parachute and covert operations training with the British Army in North Africa, the

Battalion was attached to a British Commando Unit and shipped to a partisan held Yugoslav Island (Vis) in the Adriatic Sea. The combined American and British units raided and retook many of the surrounding islands occupied by German forces. Captain Markoutsas often accompanied the raiding parties. He carried surgical equipment and medical supplies, including whole blood, with him into the fray. Without regard for his personal safety, he performed amputations, lifesaving surgical procedures and administered medical aid to the injured while in the thick of the fighting.

Smaller, battle tested Greek Battalion tactical units were soon formed. They flew over and jumped into Greece with supplies, munitions and gold for the Greek resistance fighter, "Andantes". Alongside their soul brother partisan fighters they made harassing raids against the German occupiers. Their primary task was to delay and detain the German confiscated trains, preventing them from taking food and supplies out of the country back to Germany. They blew up railroad tracks, trains, bridges, supply depots, and engaged in firefights with accompanying German security forces. Upon completion of their missions, the marauding units returned to the island of Vis by PT boats. Then, after a short-lived rest, they resupplied and returned for another intrusion. Uncle George laughingly said that he never parachuted into Greece, but he was pushed out of a plane six times.

When the war wound down in Greece, the Battalion was deployed to Italy and assisted in the liberation of that country. Uncle George oversaw the operation of a field medical unit treating both allied and prisoner personnel. His dedication to care for the injured earned him the prestigious "Legion of Merit" medal. Uncle George never offered details about his exploits and deeds. When queried his response was "We did what was necessary" and that ended the conversation.

Dad died shortly after the war. Mom was faced with the challenge of raising two small children alone. When she called her brother to express concerns about her children's ills, Uncle George was there with his little black bag. He was more than a doctor and uncle. He became our mentor, surrogate father and inspiration.

Dino was fascinated with Uncle George's little black bag, and he soon had one of his own. It was complete with gauze, tape, bandages and tongue depressors. The prize content, however, was an assortment of used glass tube hypodermic syringes. When not used for playing doctor, the larger ones made excellent squirt guns. Dino still cherishes one of Uncle George's black bags given to him when he graduated from Loyola Medical School.

Another hand-me-down to Dino was a bruised black case containing an old microscope and some glass specimen slides. In the case was Uncle George's instrument used during his medical school training. Dino used it for pathology class. A significant, startling discovery was made when Dino examined the slides. Uncle George had purposely included slides of our Father's pathology study among the other specimens. They clearly showed the cells that had invaded Dad's lungs, first thought to be cancer, but were actually sarcomas. For Dino to actually see what caused our father's death was not only traumatic but another subtle lesson from Uncle George. He orchestrated the transformation of a microscope into a humanizing instrument.

As was the practice of the time, Uncle George oversaw the removal of our tonsils. He administered necessary vaccinations and bandaged our cuts and wounds. When asked to give us pain medicine to soothe the aches and pains his reply was, "I'll give you Bulgarian Anesthesia." When we asked, "What's that Uncle George?" he replied, "NOTHING". He knew from his military experience that the long term effects of the pain killers were worse than enduring temporary discomfort. That lesson, explained in Uncle George's lecture mode, emphasized enduring short term discomforts for long term gains.

Uncle George, as hinted to above, was a gifted

psychiatrist. He stressed being responsible for one's personal decisions, actions and the subsequent consequences. Another case in point: Dino worked in the warehouse of the Atlas Prager Brewery when he returned from his first year in college. It was hard labor hauling heavy wooden cases of beer onto delivery trucks. The next summer, with two years of pre-med under his belt, Dino asked Uncle George if he could find him a job working as an orderly in a hospital. "Of course I can," was the reply, "But I won't. I want you to go back to the Brewery for another year. I want you to appreciate what people endure while making a living; and don't you forget that when treating your patients." That made the task in the brewery much more than just a job. It became another lesson in life.

Uncle George was a member of the dying breed of "*Physicians and Surgeons*". That was written on his office door. Doctors of that era did everything. There was not a procedure he was afraid to undertake. Specialization became the norm in medicine after the war, and Uncle George eventually became a Family practitioner. However, he often scrubbed in when a patient of his was undergoing surgery and engaged in long hours of conversation with Dino regarding new surgical techniques. In his heart he never left the challenge of the operating room or, for that matter, the battle field.

THE MENTOR

Another Saturday night, and little did Dino realize that this evening would change his life forever.

Other young fellows looked forward to Saturday evenings with anticipation of adventure and new conquests. Dino anticipated either boredom or emergencies and panic too bizarre to comprehend. Typically, the life of a second year Med Student involves long hours, tedious study, and a lack of sleep. These were compounded by a lack of money. This necessitated his occasional weekend job as an Extern working in the emergency room at Swedish Covenant Hospital. This was an opportunity to learn medicine hands-on without professors breathing down his neck. Fortunately, he lived just down the block and around the corner from the hospital. Little time was lost traveling, and being close to home and Mom's cooking made the job bearable.

The emergency area was an isolated part of the hospital. Rarely did the attending staff venture there unless called in for a specific need. Typical maladies were treated by the ER staff and patients were then released with the assurance that all would soon be well.

Fracture and break cases were kept in waiting rooms until weekend orthopedic surgeons on call came in to set and cast them. Trauma cases involving accidents, however, were a bigger challenge. Often speed was the main factor determining survival. Rapid diagnoses made in the ER determined who was to administer the task of keeping a patient alive. Seriously injured patients left the ER on a gurney for admittance into the mysterious bowels of the hospital. It was highly unusual for the extern to follow-up or to see patients for treatment after they were wheeled out of the area.

Idle periods might have been boring for others, but to Dino they were a Godsend. He was pursuing a Master's degree in Physiology in addition to his studies to attain his Medical Degree. Instead of cat napping, he worked on his additional coursework. As chance would have it, one evening while reading about heart and vascular aneurisms, he was called to examine a new arrival.

A tall thin fellow, about sixty-five years old, was brought in exhibiting great discomfort. The man was ushered into an examining room and placed onto a gurney. Ashen, and with a faint pulse, he was in fact dying. Observing the patient and recalling what he had just read, Dino called for a surgeon to come immediately.

Dr. Thomas G. Baffes was on the way out of the

hospital and en route to his car. After a day of surgery, he was on his way home. Baffes heard the commotion and yelling and ran into the examining room. Dino had never seen him before. The doctor looked more like a retired football player than a physician. Portly, slightly rumpled, yet intense in a friendly way, he exuded a persona of confidence and of being in complete control.

As the doctor entered the room, Dino explained the situation and said that the patient's wife had told him that her husband had a history of an abdominal aortic aneurism.

After one look at the patient, Dr. Baffes asked Dino for a knife. He removed his suit jacket and rolled up his shirt sleeves, then pulled the patient's upper clothing off, exposing his chest. Without a moment's pause, Dr. Baffes plunged the knife into the comatose man's belly. Blood spurted out, flowing everywhere. Reaching into the now opened cavity, he knew exactly where to locate the burst aorta. He found the leak and pinched it shut with his bare muscular hand.

Calm as a person waiting for a book in the library, Dr. Baffes told Dino to call the operating room. He asked that someone bring a vascular clamp to replace his fingers on the rupture and relayed instructions to the surgical suite to prepare it for the repair procedure. "Have you ever seen a ruptured aneurism being repaired?" he asked Dino. After the negative response, Dr. Baffes said, "Come upstairs with me and see how we do it." They proceeded to the operating suites, changed into scrubs, washed together and walked side by side into another world.

The patient had been draped and prepared for surgery. As they entered the room, Dr. Baffes described in detail what was to take place, and more importantly, why. Since the initial incision had been made in an unsterile environment with an unclean instrument, it was important that all possible sources of infection be eliminated. Thus, the cavity and all exposed organs were flushed continually with a heparin sterilizing solution. More time was spent in the flushing procedure than during the actual surgery. **Lesson one: Do everything possible to eliminate the chance of infection.** Next, the emergency vascular clamp was repositioned to allow more room for the procedure. **Lesson two: give yourself enough room to do your work in a clear area.**

The procedure began as Dr. Baffes made a long slit in the aorta at the site of the rupture. The walls of the aneurism were then rolled back to expose the inside of the aneurism cavity. A few moments were taken to clean debris from the area before taking the next step. Dr. Baffes had asked that a few Dacron graft tubes of various sizes be saturated in sterile solution as part of the preparation procedure. **Lesson three: have enough available supplies on hand to never be caught short with the wrong size.** Selecting one that would fit, he placed one end of the tube in the cavity and inserted it slightly inside the exposed opening of the aorta on one side of the cavity. Likewise, the other end of the tube was then inserted into the aorta opening on the other side. Thus, a connecting tube was in place to allow unobstructed blood flow through the aorta at the site of the former aneurism.

The Dacron tube was sutured into place; the flaps of

the aneurism wall were wrapped over and around the tube and likewise sutured to cover the repair. Vascular clamps were removed, flow was restarted through the repair zone, and the area was checked for leakage. Finding none, the cavity was closed. **Lesson four: be sure that all work is completed and inspected before closing.** Dino was awed by the sure "flying fingers" of the surgeon. He had never before witnessed such competence in action.

What a life-changing experience! This doctor, calm, cool, and with a focused purpose, had just saved a man's life before Dino's very eyes. No regard for time, clothing, location; just the confidence to do his job skillfully and efficiently. Dino knew then and there that he must become a cardiovascular surgeon. Dr. Baffes sensed the student's enthusiasm to become a part of what was just witnessed. The doctor was also impressed that an extern had made the correct diagnosis that had allowed him to intercede without hesitation. Perhaps Dino belonged next to him at the table in the OR. An instant bond was made that would last for years to come.

Thomas G. Baffes, MD, the son of an immigrant Greek Hot Dog Vender in New Orleans, graduated first in his class from Tulane University Medical School in 1945. After years of training and teaching, Tom came to Chicago in 1952 to work as an associate of Dr. Willis J. Potts, surgeon-in-chief at Children's Memorial Hospital. Under the guidance of Dr. Potts, Dr. Stanley Gibson, a clinical cardiologist, and Dr. Joseph Boggs, head of pathology, Dr. Baffes developed and perfected a surgical procedure known as "Transposition of the Great Vessels". This life saving operation gave hope to previously doomed children born with congenital deformed hearts. Along with Dr. Potts, the team of Dr. Baffes, Dr. Arthur DeBeers and Dr. William L. Ricker performed hundreds of life changing "Blue Baby" transformation corrections. These four doctors were truly among the pioneers of pediatric cardiovascular surgery. Dr. Baffes eventually became the

Chairman of the Department of Surgery at Mt Sinai Hospital in Chicago. He finished his career by retiring from medicine and becoming, again first in his class, a successful Trial Attorney specializing, naturally, in Medical Malpractice cases.

Dino succeeded in his quest and became a cardiovascular surgeon. Years later he became the Chief of the Department of Cardiovascular Surgery at Cook County Hospital in Chicago. County Hospital was an Acute Trauma facility with ambulances, police cars, and walk-in patients continuously filling the emergency room. Benches lining the hallways were never empty of the bedraggled, the weary, and the walking wounded waiting to be examined. Because of the very nature of this emergency room, doctors of all stripes and specialties were perpetually in and out of the area. Unlike the old days at Swedish Covenant, there were never idle moments. Heart surgeons from the cardiovascular department could often be found there as quick responders to the not unusual cases of bullet or knife wounds to the chest.

On one occasion Dino went to the ER to check on his team of doctors. While there he passed a struggling person waiting to be admitted. That same instant diagnosis flashed into his head. All the examining rooms were occupied, and there was not a vacant spot on the hallway line of benches. Dino gently placed the fellow on the hallway floor, and while proceeding to pull off his shirt called out, "Quick, someone bring me a knife!" Of course, the rest of the story was told in the overseeing shadow of Dr. Baffes.

AHEPA and the HUNTA

Children, compassion, charity, contributions, corrections, cures, comfort, congratulations—coup, control, conceit, cancel! The letter "C" tells it all.

"Tha Pethani". (The baby is going to die) A young mother in Greece had heard those tragic words from her doctor. "The heart is deformed." The sympathetic but frustrated doctor knew nothing medically was available to him to save the child's life. "What can I do?" she asked. "I don't know; why don't you take the baby to America?" was the reply.

The strong-willed mother's instinct kicked in. She did call America. She heard there was a Greek doctor in Chicago who operated on babies. Was there any way to contact him? Who might intercede for her? Would he offer to help? How could she get there if he would help? What would it cost? Insurmountable obstacles, to be sure, but she had to save her child.

AHEPA (*American Hellenic Educational Progressive Association*) members in Chicago heard about her dilemma. The Greek educational and philanthropic organization existed for just such an opportunity to assist. Dr. Thomas Baffes was contacted. Of course he would help, and at no cost. He also made arrangements for Augustana Hospital to provide its facilities for free. Transportation by a Greek shipping line was obtained for the trip to New York, and an airline offered to fly the mother and child to Chicago. A Herculean task was accomplished in a very short time by the AHEPA volunteers. Mother and child made it safely to Chicago.

The Blue Baby operation, perfected by Dr. Baffes some years earlier at Children's Memorial Hospital, was a success. After a recuperative stay with a compassionate local family, the jubilant pair returned to Greece. Word of the miraculous lifesaving procedure performed on the previously doomed baby spread throughout Greek medical circles. (The doctors later became reluctant conduits for additional case referrals to AHEPA. They wished they instead had the facilities available to perform the procedures in Greece.)

That was in 1963. Forward to 1974: by then AHEPA had sponsored and brought over thirty-three seriously ill Greek children to Chicago. "Stash" Betzelos expanded the reach of the Heart Program when he became the District Governor of AHEPA in 1966-67. The 13th District Lodge, many Ahepans including his brother, Jim, and their wives Irene and Persey, sparked the full support of the membership. Affairs were held to raise money. Transportation from Greece was procured and sponsors found to chaperon the patients' families. But most importantly, the doctors were firmly committed. Not only did they give their services gratis, but they also convinced the hospitals to provide operating facilities at little or no cost for these cases.

While still a resident, Dino assisted Dr. Baffes in the operating room with the AHEPA children. In addition to Augustana Hospital, many operations were also performed at Swedish Covenant Hospital. By the end of the program Dino, then a board certified cardiothoracic surgeon, was Chief of Surgery at Cook County Hospital. He performed some of the final AHEPA cases there. Because Cook County was a public facility, volunteer services originally created just for the Greek kids had to be offered to all nationalities. Many more heart operations were performed there on the same charitable basis to other needy children.

In 1967, the HUNTA overthrew the government of Greece by a military coup. They had control of the country during the latter period of the AHEPA Heart Program. Some of the colonels in control were not pleased that Greek children had to go to America to be treated. They wanted a heart program to be developed in Greece. No more Greek babies going to America! The AHEPA, as a last charitable gesture of their Heart Program, raised funds to purchase a heart-lung machine and had it shipped to the Evangelismos, the largest hospital in Athens.

An emissary of the HUNTA met with Dino in Chicago. He invited Dino to come to Greece to inspect their facilities, meet with the doctors there and submit a report outlining the creation of a Greek pediatric heart program. Dino remembered a young fellow from Greece that had trained as a surgical resident on Dr. Baffles' service at Children's Memorial Hospital. The doctor later returned home to Athens. He might be a good beginning point. Dino located him in Athens and called him to explain the mission. They arranged to meet when Dino arrived in Greece.

A car and driver picked up Dino at the Athens airport. They went straight to the Grande Bretagne Hotel across from Constitution Square. After getting settled in his room, Dino called the Greek doctor to let him know that he had arrived. The driver was waiting for him and informed Dino that he would be his chauffer, translator, and guide for the entire time of his stay.

After dinner, Dino excused himself to go to bed. As an aside, the driver mentioned to Dino that it would not be a good idea for Dino to get too chummy with his doctor acquaintance in Athens. Dino asked why and was informed that the doctor was sympathetic to the wrong political party. Nothing more was said, but when Dino was in the elevator something odd occurred to him. Dino had never mentioned the doctor's name! The only way that the driver could have known about him was if his phone had been tapped. That made for a fretful night, but forewarned is forearmed. The incident set the tone for a cautionary, careful and slightly uncomfortable stay. Dino realized that the driver was in reality an undercover agent.

Compulsory trips were made to various military hospital facilities with the idea that perhaps one could be converted to a heart center. Luncheons and dinners were arranged with an array of doctors and staff from some of the hospitals in Athens. Tours were conducted to showcase their operating suites, hospital wards and training programs.

Dino observed but said little. It became obvious that

the country had been ravaged by two wars and civil unrest. Little money was available to devote to modernize Greece's medical community. Many of the doctors were older gentlemen. A brain drain had robbed Greece of a rich crop of younger doctors who had trained in America, Germany, or England and never returned. It would take a lot of time and money to get something viable started.

A parting meeting was arranged with some of the colonels who were interested in Dino's report. He informed them that it would take some time to properly document his impressions and suggestions, and he would send it as soon as possible after returning to America. There was no way in hell that he was about to give them a factual, but critical, report while still in the country.

When the meeting was about to conclude one of the colonels asked Dino if he would stay another day to operate on his sister. She needed her gall bladder removed, and Dino was a famous doctor from America; he should be the one to do it. Not wanting to embarrass the colonel, Dino suggested that she instead go to an American hospital that specialized in gastric surgery. That idea was accepted; and Dino called a friend at the Cleveland Clinic and made arraignments for her to be treated there. That really made Dino look like a hero. The colonel praised him as a fine example of an American boy from good Greek stock. Dino was just glad to be going home.

Stash Betzelos, while on a trip to Greece in 1975, stopped by Evangelismos hospital to check on the AHEPA heart-lung machine. It had been shipped three months prior to his visit but had just arrived at the hospital the day before his visit. Further checking revealed that it had been held captive in a customs building waiting for someone to pay 16,000 Drachmas duty for a "Machine from America." After much time and wrangling, the hospital had reluctantly paid the duty.

Stash met with "Officials" in the Customs office. In no uncertain words he clarified that the "Machine" was a charitable donation from the ORDER OF AHEPA and had the duty rescinded. How ironic, on the day before it was delivered, the hospital's only heart-lung machine had broken down. The AHEPA, with its "Machine from America" continued to save the lives of Greek children.

A SHORT STORY

Springtime in Bavaria, the snow melting, creeks running, trees budding: what more could one ask for? A jeep entering the army base courtyard with white duffle bags in the back seat could have been the answer.

Mail call, every soldier waits for that moment to reconnect with loved ones left behind. After a week on the Czechoslovakian border playing "Cold War" with the Russians, nothing could have been more important. Sweaty clothes, dirty equipment, hot showers, all would wait until the last letter was taken out of the last bag.

"Lieutenant Tatooles, I have three for you."

One was from, mom, another from a college friend, but what's this, a letter from my brother. He never wrote; too busy studying to become a doctor. Something must be wrong. There was a slight flutter in my heart as I took my time opening the missile, fearing what it might contain.

Relief came as I read a request. Dino was one of the first medical students at Loyola University to pursue a Masters degree in Physiology at the same time he was studying to become a doctor. He said that is was exceedingly difficult to simultaneously fulfill the requirements of both courses and was looking for some help to save him precious time. The Masters program required that a language be included. He had chosen German. Dino knew that I had studied German both in High School and College. Since I had been in Germany with the army for over half a year improving my language skills, his request should be easy to fulfill.

His professor had assigned the class to write and submit a short story written in German as the final assignment of the course. Dino asked that I go to a local book store, find a book of German short stories and mail it to him. That would help him save time. He could choose a story, change it a bit, and get that pesky subject out of the way.

When the book arrived Dino chose a story, altered it, or so he thought, and submitted it. A few days later his paper was returned. In big red letters across the first page, the professor had written THE AUTHOR GETS AN A+, YOU GET AN F! Dino had chosen, unfortunately, one of the most famous stories written as his submission.

The understanding professor heard the story, laughed, but gave no quarter. Dino would have to take an oral exam in two weeks to prove that he had a working knowledge of the language. The pressure was now even greater than before because he had to pass the test to receive his Master's degree. Remembering a friend that frequented "Zum Deutschen Ek", a local German restaurant, a call was made, arrangements completed and Dino had his supper there every night for the following two weeks. Waiters, along with the friend, immersed him in German until he was dreaming it.

The professor was informed of the unique tutoring arrangement and he was convinced to give Dino the oral exam in a back room of the restaurant. Needless to say, all worked out well. In piecemeal German, Dino ordered food and drinks for all. His German language skills might not have been great, but the food was delicious, which was apparently enough to get him his diploma. The pirated short story soon became another short story.

GETTING PERSONAL

The operating room can mimic a stage play. It might feature a mystery, a drama, a tragedy, a beautiful love story, or even a comedy.

*I*f there ever was a person exhibiting the classic Napoleonic complex, it surely was Dr. Hadrold C. Voris, a neurosurgeon at Mercy Hospital in Chicago. He was a highly respected surgeon in a demanding specialty. Teaching others was as strong a passion for Dr. Voris, as was the perfection he demanded of those working with him. The only small thing about the doctor was his stature; everything else was big, loud and commanding. Dr. Voris always had the lead role in whatever he was doing.

When Dino was a second year medical student he was assigned to train with Dr. Voris. He recalled that while making rounds, the doctor wore a large athletic warm-up jacket with his initials, H.C.V., monogrammed in big letters on the back. Dr. Voris was brutally hard on the student trainees assigned to him because, as he pointed out, "There is no room for errors in neurosurgery!" A favorite tactic was to wait until the group making rounds with him was at the apex of joining hallways before he started the loud, harsh grilling of his students. Thus, everyone on the floor was within earshot of the embarrassment dealt out to an unprepared student. Attention getting, crude? Yes, but it was a very effective teaching tool.

On a day that Dr. Voris was scheduled to perform the removal of a glioblastoma (brain tumor), Dino was assigned to assist in the operation. A young scrub nurse in training, recently elevated to the rank of surgical nurse, joined in the cast that was to perform the ensuing drama. The unfortunate neophyte surgical nurse was struck by the severity of her first solo performance. That, compounded with the realization that the star of the show was a demanding and unforgiving tyrant, gave her stage fright and put her into a near panic.

Her timing was off, and the wrong instruments were being placed in the surgeon's hand. Things were either misplaced or dropped. Dr. Voris started to sweat profusely as he struggled to complete the delicate task at hand and was becoming more exasperated by the minute with the now traumatized young lady. No need to shout any more. The doctor fought the procedure to a successful completion and rushed to the doctor's room to shower and cool off.

Realizing the stress she had caused, the nurse waited by the doctor's room to apologize to Dr. Voris when he came out. The phone started to ring. Wishing to help make up for her past inadequacy, she entered the doctor's room to answer the phone. At that same moment Dr. Voris, stark naked, also came out of the shower to answer the phone. He looked her in the eye, uttered a sigh and said in a loud booming voice for all to hear, "From now on you can call me Harold!"

Some plays have surprise endings.

ROUNDS

Caring for those that care for us...

Great Uncle John G. Tatooles was short, stout, and roly-poly. From a distance his silhouette might have looked like an oversized beach ball. He was the proverbial Mr. five-by-five. Uncle John, the youngest brother of our grandfather, once had a restaurant on the south side of Chicago, across the street from Mercy Hospital. He never married, devoting his life to the store. As he and the neighborhood aged, the restaurant was eventually closed and Uncle John downsized to a portable Hot Dog and Tamale stand hitched behind his old Plymouth coupe.

His daily routine never varied. For six days a week, after reading the stock pages and finishing his morning toast and coffee, Uncle John went down to the garage behind his bachelor apartment. He lit his propane hot dog and bun steamers, loaded the canopied trailer with the day's provisions and drove a few blocks to the street-side curb near the R. R. Donnelly Company printing plant employee entrance. Along with a few dozen drive-bys, the twelve story structure provided enough hungry personnel to keep him busy throughout the day. If the weather merited it, Uncle John later spent the early evening hours alongside the lakefront parkways until his supplies were depleted. Uncle John did all-right for himself.

Sundays were devoted to visiting with family and friends. That seemed to be the only time he could partake of a nutritious meal. Never cooking at home, one has to assume that his diet consisted of hot dogs, polish sausages, tamales and soda pop. Not hard to explain how he came by his rotund physique.

We all knew where to find him. It was a real treat to visit with our sweet, kind, unique relative. After the usual greeting, Uncle John always told us, "Don't have a hot dog, have a polish!" That was offering us the *best in the house*. For most of us the visits were few and far between. Since the stand was not all that far from the University of Chicago hospital, Dino had a greater opportunity to stop by for his polish. Uncle John had a great respect for people in the medical profession. Back in the days of his restaurant many of his customers and friends were doctors. That made his nephew, *Doctor* Dino Tatooles, something special.

One day, Dino passed by looking for the hot dog stand. Uncle John was not around. Concerned about the aging fellow, Dino went to Uncle John's apartment house where he found a sickly aging gentleman lying uncomfortably on his bed. After an interesting conversation, Dino convinced the tired old man to go to the University of Chicago Hospital for a check-up. A deal was struck; Uncle John would go as long as he was under Dino's care. A slight problem: Dino's service was in the Cardiac unit.

Uncle John was round. There are many other forms of rounds. A round of drinks, rounds of ammunition, golf rounds to name a few. The medical profession also lays claim to a few forms of *rounds*.

Historically, medicine was taught by having students make the "rounds" of patients while tagging behind a doctor and simply observing. In the middle 1800s, a formal Grand Round was established. Patients were wheeled into an amphitheater gallery with the medical students and observers seated in semi-circular fashion looking down from above. A formally dressed doctor would enter, establish his superior position to the group, and proceed to lecture to the audience. With little or no regard for the patient's thoughts or feelings, the doctor would go into detail describing history, treatment, and prognosis of the person before them. Some doctors accepted questions, but most assumed that the students were inferior and not yet worthy of attention. Prior to the age of sterilization, some surgeons even proudly wore blood encrusted jackets when they lectured as evidence of the many operations they had performed.

Advancing forward a hundred years, medicine is still being taught with rounds. Grand Rounds have been humanized and still performed by heads of departments or invited guest lecturers to groups of interested attendees. Lecture halls have taken the place of the amphitheater, although some still do exist. These rounds may be weekly, monthly, or anytime a department head wishes to schedule one.

More common is the daily case round. A group of residents, interns and students follow the attending doctor as he visits each of the patients in his service at the start of the day. After a stop at the patient's room, they might gather out of earshot in the corridor, review the chart workup, and go through a question and answer session as part of the teaching process. Often this is also repeated at the end of the day. An extension of the case round is the coffee round where cases are discussed during coffee breaks.

Shortly after admitting Uncle John to the cardiac service, Dino was conducting rounds with a group of the usual residents, interns and medical students. Dr. William Adams, Chief of Surgery, elected to join them that day. Dr. Adams had an unusual bedside manner. Upon entering a patient's room he pulled up a chair and sat next to the patient. Chatting amicably with the person, you would think that it was just two people talking after a long lost time apart. After a while Adams would excuse himself and out the door he would go, leaving the patient sorry to see the doctor leave.

Finishing his friendly chat with Uncle John, Dr. Adams left the room and immediately turned to Dino. "This is a cardiac unit. Why on earth is this person on this floor? And what does the condition obese and shortness of breath mean?" Dino explained that Uncle John was his uncle, a bachelor, and in need of some long overdue medical attention. Dino had Uncle John there to personally care for him. Adams replied, "I see from our chat that he thinks the world of you and would follow anything that you asked him to do. What do you have in mind?"

Dino reviewed the case: Uncle John was grossly overweight, had poor nutrition, deteriorating muscle tone, and a slight state of depression. The course of treatment was as follows: 1) Put him on a 700 calorie a day diet; 2) Start him on a course of physical therapy; and 3) Have him visit with a psychiatrist. Dino wanted the best treatment possible for his uncle.

Dr. Adams looked at Dino, making sure he had the attention of the entire entourage, and then asked, "Do you really love your uncle?"

"Yes, of course", he replied.

"What is his main source of enjoyment and pleasure at this stage of his life?"

Dino replied, "Obviously, he loves eating, and checking his stocks and thinking about his family."

"And you, doctor, who says that he loves this man, are going to take away his greatest pleasure, torture him with exercise and embarrass him with the introduction of a psychiatrist? Is that how to treat an eighty-four-year-old who may not have much longer to live?"

Dr. Adams' wisdom was obvious to all who were present. There is medical treatment and compassionate treatment. In this case the best treatment was love and concern. Simply the fact that his nephew was caring for him made Uncle John soon well enough to leave the hospital and go back to selling his hot dogs for a few more years.

What goes around eventually becomes part of a round.

ON THE JOB TRAINING

Dino was the senior surgical resident on Dr. Block's service. Others viewed him more as a protégée. There was a certain unspoken trusting relationship between them.

$\mathcal{A}$ short, rather stout lady scheduled for an adrenalectomy was the first case of the day. Prior to today's laparoscopy procedures, the operation typically involved removal of a portion of a rib to get at the adrenal gland. A patient was positioned face down in a prone position on the operating table and was slightly bent to provide better access to the back portion of the rib cage. The adrenal gland would be found under the twelfth rib.

Dr. Block instructed Dino to start the case. He would come in later to see how things were progressing. Dino made a thorough study of the situation before proceeding. In this case, because the patient was inordinately short and overweight, Dino suspected that the anatomy might not be normal. A study of x-rays confirmed his suspicion; the adrenal gland in this person was under the eleventh rib, not the twelfth.

The patient was positioned on the operating table, draped, and ready for the procedure to begin. Dino scrubbed and, with scalpel in hand, marked and made the first incision. Dr. Block came in to observe his trainee. He placed a stool right behind his resident and watched.

After a while he asked, "Are you sure that you are at the twelfth rib?"

"No", Dino replied, "I'm cutting out the eleventh rib."

"Are you stupid? Don't you know that it has to be the twelfth?" And with that, he bopped Dino on the side of the head. "You are screwing up, big time!"

Dino continued as if not hearing a word, which prompted more bopping and more berating.

The site was opened and Dino asked for the saw. Blocked started at him again. "You can't cut out the eleventh rib; it has to be the twelfth." More bopping and cursing his resident, who was supposed to know what he was doing. "I told you to stop, you ignoramus." (Actually, slightly different words were used.) The cut was completed, the rib removed. All that was left to do was slit open the underlying membrane.

Dino made an incision, spread apart the membrane and stepped back for Dr. Block to see. The adrenal gland was directly in front of him, in the abnormal location directly beneath the spot where the eleventh rib had been removed. When Block saw that he said, "I was just testing you; I wanted to see how much faith and belief you had in yourself."

When they left the doctor's locker room, Dr. Block put his arm around Dino and said, "You did a great job this morning, came through with flying colors. I was testing you to see how much confidence you had in yourself. I might have over done it a bit, but if one is not sure of what he is doing in the operating room, then he doesn't belong there!"

THE NOTEBOOK

Some people could not live without it; she was one of them. The notebook of an anal-oriented patient helped her dutifully follow her doctor's instructions to the letter. It was the liberating source of relief from constant pain and probably the most important item in her possession.

The University of Chicago Hospital and Medical Center has long been known for its excellence in patient care. Coupled with hospital staff, much of the recognition is justifiably attributed to an outstanding teaching faculty. One of the academics was the renowned Dr. George Block, professor of surgery. The scion of a vast family fortune, Dr. Block could have pursued any pastime in the world, but nothing pleased him more than operating, providing for the welfare of his patients, and teaching. He also was constantly relating patient histories to his young entourage of surgical trainees in order to humanize and personalize medicine. The patient, not the procedure, had to be the most important consideration.

After making his morning rounds, Dr. Block and his group of junior and senior residents, Dino included, took a break for coffee. It was there that the best stories were told. Dr. Block often included histories provided to him by other professors. One such tale from his friend, Dr. Joseph B. Kirsner, professor of gastroenterology, will never be forgotten.

Dr. Kirsner was world famous for his treatments of colon-related disorders. Many of these maladies had stress and mind-driven factors as components of the condition. Kirsner perfected a technique of having his patients transfer their thoughts away from the colon and into notebook entries. Everything related to their colon had to be recorded in their notebook. Food eaten and consequences of the diet, flatulence, bowel movements, color and consistency of the stool and any other significant event had to be noted as to time, place, and feeling.

Dr. Kirsner met with his patients weekly to review the contents of their notebooks. His technique of transference made the notebook more important than the underlying condition. It did wonders for the relief of pain and led to many referrals from his satisfied patients. Many were women from the North Shore of Chicago who didn't mind the long trip down to the south side and the University of Chicago.

Dr. Block related to the group a history told to him by Dr. Kirsner concerning one of those North Shore ladies. She had been almost fanatical with the entries to her notebook. One day, while shopping downtown at Marshall Field's department store, she was suddenly taken by a violent gastric rush. Racing to the woman's lounge she found all the stalls occupied. Panic overtook her and screams of instant need were uttered. A little girl in one of the stalls became frightened and finished up to let the frantic lady have the space. By chance, the toddler had a little balloon with her. In her haste to get out she did not notice that the little balloon had fallen into the commode.

Thankful for the now-available facility, the woman dashed into the stall and, without looking, sat down and proceeded to get relief. Feeling better, she looked down to observe the toilet's contents. After which she would record the result into her notebook. She shrieked with terror at the sight. Never in her life had she seen anything so disturbing. She needed to know, immediately, what had just transpired.

In those days Marshall Field's had an on-duty medical staff to meet the needs of its customers. Remembering this, the woman closed the door of the stall, shouted that no one should enter, and then proceeded to find medical help.

A kindly, older retired Doctor who was working part time at Field's came to the rest room. He patiently listened to the woman's recent ordeal and attempted to comfort the harried lady. Proceeding to the stall in question, with her in tow, he peered into the bowl and saw the floating brown mound.

Years of diagnosis prompted him to attempt to bring some sort of order to the situation before him. Opening his jacket, he reached into the vest pocket and pulled out a worn old leather comb case. On the side of the case was a slit containing a nail file. Taking the file in hand, he proceeded to probe the brown mass. The inevitable happened; there was a muffled explosion and excrement flew all over the place.

The woman's terror now was magnified a hundredfold. The splattered doctor exited the stall and exploded into uproarious laughter. Now further unnerved, she yelled, "Doctor, what in the world is the matter?"

He replied, "Lady, I have been practicing medicine for the past fifty years, and this is the first time that I have ever seen a fart!"

Who says medical histories are boring?

DR. COLLER'S GIFT OF A LIFETIME

Imagine auditioning for plays on Broadway, movies in Hollywood, and a few TV and radio spots thrown into the mix, all at the same time. A callback has proven your merit. You have been selected to perform with all the top stars in their own venues.

*I*n 1920, Dr. Fredrick A. Coller left Harvard to head the department of cardiovascular surgery at the University of Michigan in Ann Arbor. A brilliant surgeon and a dedicated academic, Dr. Coller started teaching when studies and new treatments of the heart were virtually exploding. Top practitioners were engrossed in studies dear to their hearts (pun intended) throughout the country.

Dr. John Gibbon had developed an early version of the heart-lung machine in Philadelphia. In Minneapolis, C. Walt Lillehei's daring new techniques revolutionized the field of heart surgery. Alfred Blalock performed miracles on blue babies at Johns Hopkins, while at the Mayo clinic Dr. John Kirklin was the first to be routinely performing open heart operations using an improved heart lung machine. Out west in Portland, Oregon, Albert Starr started installing his artificial heart valves, and at Stanford Dr. Norman Shumway advanced the development of heart transplantation. In Texas, Dr. Michael DeBakey was creating innovative vascular surgical techniques while his former colleague, Dr. Denton Cooley, made his mark perfecting by-pass operations at his Texas Heart Institute.

To obtain an all-encompassing vision of the rapidly changing heart field, extensive time and travel would be required to permit observation of each star surgeon in his native surrounding. Envisioning such a vehicle to accomplish this "Super Grand Round", Dr. Coller created and endowed the Dr. F. A. Coller Clinical Tour. It provided outstanding surgical residents in their last two years of training the opportunity to spend a month observing and working with their chosen "idols".

Dr. George Block, Dino's Chief during his years of residency at the University of Chicago, was a former student of Dr. Coller at the University of Michigan. Dr. Block was also a devoted supporter of Dr. Coller's philanthropies. When Dino started his second year, Dr. Block suggested that Dino apply for a Clinical Tour Fellowship. This award is normally given yearly to eight recipients. In 1967, due to a financial shortfall, just one award was granted. A few months later, Dr. Block was overjoyed that his resident had been selected as the only Coller fellow for that year. Selections of medical centers to visit, doctors to see and procedures to observe were submitted to the society, approved, and the life-altering journey was ready to commence.

Dr. Dwight McGoon

First stop was the famous clinic in Rochester, Minnesota, founded by the brothers Mayo. Open heart procedures were becoming routine there as a result of Dr. John Kirklin's work to improve the heart lung machine. Kirklin and his resident Albert Pacifico, left Mayo to start a world renowned school at the University of Alabama, leaving Dr. Dwight McGoon in charge. Dino met with Dr. McGoon, observed open heart surgery, made rounds together and was introduced to the implementation of post-op intensive care treatment. Years later, Dino operated with Dr. McGoon and Dr. Pacifico at the Clinic in Bergamo, Italy.

Dr. Clarence Walton Lillehei

Next stop was the University of Minnesota. The famous, or infamous, Dr. C. Walton "Walt" Lillehei, a bold and innovative maverick, was taking heart surgery down a path where others dared not venture. Dr. Lillehei performed heart surgery by using hypothermia and cross-circulation techniques before heart lung machines were available. He also was responsible for the development and installation of the first wearable external pacemaker, and a myriad of other medical devices. (The first totally implantable pacemaker was performed by Ake Senning at the Karolinska Institute in Stockholm, Sweden.) As a clinical professor, he taught and trained the doctors who first performed heart transplants.

What an awe inspiring opportunity to observe Dr. Lillehei's surgical wizardry and to follow him as he made his rounds. Dino and Walt eventually became close friends and enjoyed a few cocktails together at many medical conventions.

Returning to the University of Chicago, Dino spent time with Dr. Block relating and discussing the myriad new procedures he had observed. A few more weeks of residency and he was ready for the major leg of his tour out west. It began with a stop at the University of Washington in Seattle to visit Dr. K. Alvin Merendino, chief of surgery.

Dr. K. Alvin Merendino

Dr. Merendino graduated from Yale in 1940, and then went to the University of Minnesota, where he received a Ph.D. in Surgery. A "Do Everything" surgeon, he migrated to the cardiac field because it was interesting and difficult. Open heart operations using an improved but still primitive heart lung oxygenator were a challenge. Merendino felt he could do better. He left Minnesota and moved to the University of Washington. A graduate engineering student, Wayne Quinton, helped the doctor build a much improved heart lung machine. In 1956, Dr. Merendino used his modified machine to perform the first open heart operation west of Minnesota.

Dino's day stared by observing Dr. Merendino perform an open heart operation. After making rounds, the two doctors met for lunch. Dino would then normally review the day, ask questions and take notes. Dr. Merendino had other ideas. He did a reverse interview, asking deep insightful questions of the visitor. Dino was truly moved by this surgeon's ability to make him mentally explore medical areas never before contemplated.

Dr. Albert Starr

Innovation was the theme for this trip. Albert Starr was another doctor trained in the east who went west to open new territories. He bought a commercially available heart lung machine and used it to develop a significant surgical center at the University of Oregon in Portland. Prior to that time western patients were going to either Mayo or to the University of Minnesota for their procedures.

Lady luck smiled on Dr. Starr the day that a retired mechanical engineer dropped in looking for something to do. Lowell Edwards had developed a fuel injection system used in fighter planes during the Second World War that made him a multimillionaire. He was looking to use his inventive talents to develop medical devices. Together, Dr. Starr and Lowell Edwards developed the "Starr-Edwards" artificial mitral valve. Hundreds of thousands of those valves have been installed in damaged hearts and constantly improving models are being installed worldwide even today. The Edwards Laboratories continued to turn out new and innovative medical devices.

Dino found Dr. Starr to be a very friendly person, informative and entertaining. The day was started observing the doctor installing his mitral valve devices and performing other open heart operations. Then rounds and the requisite lunch, but that was not all. Dr. Starr invited Dino to join him for dinner. Dino learned that the doctor had become immensely wealthy from the devices he developed with Edwards. Surprisingly, during the course of conversation, Dr. Starr informed Dino that he was a close acquaintance of our cousin, Dr. James Tatoulis, a cardiovascular surgeon at the University of Melbourne in Australia.

Ironically, Dr. Starr developed coronary artery disease and he too needed an open heart operation. After a fleeting thought about going back east to a "big name" surgeon, he had the procedure successfully performed in his newly created facility. That helped to stem the tide of eastbound patients.

Dr. Norman E. Shumway

Dino arrived at Stanford University in Palo Alto, California, in late afternoon. He joined Dr. Shumway and his trainees making rounds at the end of the day. A friendly face was waiting in the group. Dr. Pat Daly had been an intern at Chicago, and had left the previous year to become a surgical resident under Dr. Shumway at Stanford. Pat made Dino feel at home. Pat and Thomas J. Fogarty, an associate of Dino's at the Heart Institute, eventually partnered in a most successful cardiac surgical group practice in Palo Alto.

Dr. Shumway escorted Dino into his office, but instead of the usual interview, he also invited Dino to join him for supper. What an opportunity to spend an extraordinary evening with the world famous heart transplant doctor. Shumway was an unusual chief. He believed in training his surgical residents with immediate hands on experiences rather than by them just watching him operate. He liked to say that he was the world's greatest first assistant.

Shumway came from the University of Minnesota. He had trained under Dr. C. Walt Lillehei, as did Dr. Christiaan Barnard of Cape Town, South Africa, and Christian Cabol from Paris. These three, along with Richard Lower in Richmond, Virginia, who was trained by a Lillehei trainee, became the forerunners of heart transplantation surgery in the world. Dr. Barnard performed the first human heart transplant in Cape Town, South Africa on December 3, 1967. Dr. Shumway did not perform his first transplant until January 6, 1968. Most historians agree that Shumway developed the methodology and should have been the first to perform this surgery. Legal constraints rather than medical considerations caused the delay. Previously, death was defined to occur when the heart stopped beating. If a beating heart was removed from a body to be transplanted, then the doctor could be accused of murder. Prosecutors savored the idea of having them arrested. It wasn't until 1974 that a California court finally clarified and legalized the concept of brain death.

The following morning Dino accompanied Dr. Shumway into the operating suites. This required passing through the patient waiting room area. A woman from a prominent family confronted the doctor. "My husband is undergoing open heart surgery in there and you are supposed to be doing the procedure, so why are you out here?" A few words were exchanged, and then they left and were soon scrubbed and observing Dr. Shumway's well-trained students at work. Dr. Shumway proved to be irreverent, witty, and fun to be with in the operating room. In spite of being the father of heart transplant surgery and a world renowned personality, he was also a very humble person.

Dr. Michael DeBakey

Dino was picked up at the Houston airport by Dr. Edward B. (Ted) Diethrich. Dr. Diethrich was a Michigan graduate, had studied under Dr. Coller, and was a Coller Fellow. This was the ironic beginning of their lifelong friendship. Ted took the Coller Tour recipient directly to the Baylor Medical Center and up to Dr. Michael DeBakey's office. The doctor, smaller than originally perceived, wore a white jacket over his scrubs, cap still tightly on his head. He appeared like a fireman ready to rush into the operating room at a moment's notice. After talking for about half an hour, Dr. DeBakey said that his next procedure was ready and asked Dino to scrub and join him in the OR. Dino spent the rest of the day there.

Dr. Michael "Mike" DeBakey, born of Lebanese immigrant parents, graduated from Tulane University. He spent a few early years training in France and Germany, which may have been the geneses of his rigid, stern, perfectionism and autocratic demeanor. His specialty was vascular surgery, and he was known as the person who "wrote the book" on aneurisms. Dr. DeBakey also had an intense interest in the development of artificial hearts. These devices led to the eventual schism with his associate Dr. Denton Cooley.

After a long day with Dr. DeBakey and Dr. Dierhrich in the operating room, Dino was invited to stay at Dr. Dierhrich's home. That evening Houston was playing UCLA in basketball. Amongst the few guests invited to watch the game was Dr. Denton Cooley. Cooley played varsity basketball and was an avid Houston fan. Bets were wagered. All but Dino were Houston fans. UCLA won, Dino won. Dino met with Dr. Cooley the next morning after taking money from him the night before. They, also, became very close friends.

Dr. Denton Cooley

Denton and Dino experienced an instant bonding. Providence may have had them meet the night before. One bit of advice that Denton gave to Dino was for him to spend some time training in Europe. Following that advice, Dino later spent a year at The Hospital for Sick Children in London. During the course of their time together they met with one of Dino's college Sigma Nu fraternity brothers, Herb Smith, who was a medical illustrator at Baylor. Time was also spent with Dr. Diethrich, who would eventually leave Houston and go to Arizona to form the Arizona Heart Institute. Years later, Dino was operated on at the Institute for an abdominal aneurism.

Dino observed Dr. Cooley perform ten operations in a row. His lunch break was with a dinner pail in his office so as not to be too far from the OR. Dr. Cooley had operated on more heart patients than any other surgeon in the world. It started at Johns Hopkins Medical School, where Denton finished first in his class. He was a resident under the renowned surgeon Dr. Alfred Blalock and assisted him in the first successful operation performed on a blue baby (tetralogy of Fallot). He eventually joined Dr. DeBakey in Houston and worked together with him for eighteen years. Another surgeon once said that when they worked together it was "like watching an octopus operate. There were hands everywhere." Denton was gifted with a natural surgical dexterity that made him one of the best surgeons anywhere. His demeanor was diametrically opposite DeBakey's. Always pleasant, he was at easy and in control even in the most difficult circumstances. He had the nickname, "Dr. Wonderful."

The famous schism occurred over the use of an experimental artificial heart device. It was to be used as a stop gap in a transplant patient while waiting for a donor heart. Dr. DeBakey thought that it was not quite ready to be installed in a human, and Dr. Cooley thought otherwise. He waited until DeBakey was out of town then proceeded to install the device. The outcome was not as desired. Dr. DeBakey was understandably upset, and eventually they split over this issue. Dr. Cooley left Baylor and went across the street to start his hugely successful Texas Heart Institute. It would be another forty years before the two doctors would speak to one another again.

This trip exposed Dino to many new concepts, formed lifelong friendships, and introduced him to the leaders of his medical profession. Upon his return to the University of Chicago, Dino gave a full report to Dr. Block and made a call to Dr. Coller thanking him for this "gift of a lifetime".

SHARK HUNTING

The sportsman plays it straight. He follows a prescribed pattern of conduct conforming to the rules of the game and acts in a fair manner toward the opponent. The hunter, in contrast, has no rules; he relies on instinct, cunning and lightning fast reactions to achieve his goal.

Dino was seated next to a uniformed sailor while on a flight from Washington, DC, to Vancouver, British Columbia. He had asked the fellow passenger to join him in a drink as an icebreaker for the long trip west. "I don't believe I should, sir," said the sailor. Dino wondered why he had hesitated and asked him to explain. "Sir, I believe you are out of uniform! Can't exactly tell from your dress what's your rank or unit, and I don't know who you are, but I guess you must be an officer. As a lowly seaman, I probably shouldn't be drinking with you."

Explaining that he was a doctor in the Public Health Service and their dress was Navy Issue, Dino said that his equivalent military rank was Lieutenant Commander. He had to wear a uniform because he was on an official assignment. A group of fellow uniformed doctors stationed with him at the Heart Institute of the National Institutes of Health (part of the Public Health Service stationed in Bethesda, Maryland), were also aboard. They were traveling together to attend a meeting of the American Association of Thoracic Surgeons in Vancouver. Dino told the confused sailor that a closet full of various jackets, pants, hats and accessories was kept in their office. Since no one actually bought a personal uniform, items were borrowed to wear on an as-needed basis. Dino was late in making his selection for the trip and had to make do with what was left. Hence, the resultant version of Dino's proper dress. Thankfully, the group never had to stand for inspection.

The sailor mentioned that he had grown up around Puget Sound. He was going home on leave and to do some sport fishing. Actually, that was also a part of the doctors' travel plans. The warm Pacific currents wash into Vancouver Bay sweeping in with them a bountiful fisherman's delight, 365 days a year. How could the doctors go to the greatest year-round fishing area in the Americas and not partake? Of course, fishing was included as part (maybe the most important part) of their itinerary.

Dr. Andrew "Glenn" Morrow, the Chief of the Heart Institute, accompanied by Drs. Thomas Fogarty and Carlos Lombardo, was going to the meeting to hear one of his residents, Dino, present a paper reporting the results of their heart valve research at the Institute. Dr. Morrow had a special interest in the repair and replacement of heart valves. He emphasized research in that area by all of his residents. Aside from the presentation by their associate, there was an ulterior motive for the other two doctors to be included. Because the meeting was in Victoria, British Columbia, as lifelong avid outdoorsmen, the other two doctors *had to attend*.

Even before hotel accommodations had been completed, arrangements were made to charter a fishing boat and a guide for a few days. As the meeting was winding down, other doctors were racing off to the airport. The Heart Institute doctors raced to the docks to find their boat, the *HMS Mattlock*. This time their uniforms were jeans, boots and parkas.

Prior to that trip, Dino's vast fishing experience consisted of caching blue gills and little pan fish with worm-baited hooks from a creaky pier while vacationing with the family at Brown's Lake, Wisconsin. On rare occasions the young angler was even allowed to go out a few yards into the lake and fish from within an old leaky row boat. Going after big game fish was to be quite a different experience. Even the live fish used as bait were bigger than anything anyone ever caught in Brown's Lake.

It took about three hours of dodging salty spray to reach their first fishing spot. Poles were then hooked and baited by the guide and set in rod holders around the boat. The doctors were assigned their poles to attend. It wasn't long before poles started to bend and excitement grew as they began to reel in beautiful large fighting salmon.

By the middle of the next day Dino found the excitement had worn off and just pulling in beautiful fish became almost boring. A little dingy that the crew had used to leave the boat was tied alongside the fishing vessel. Dino spotted it and conjured thoughts of fishing from that old leaky row boat. Impulsively, or impishly, but mostly foolishly, he set his baited rod and reel into the dinghy and pushed off into the open waters.

After rowing a bit, but wise enough to stay near the big boat, Dino dropped his bait into the blue green waters and waited. WHAM! A salmon struck his line. Instead of the rod being in a holder, it was in his hands. Because he was holding the rod tightly, the jolt almost spun him off the dinghy. Now the fish had his attention. Another even stronger tug jolted Dino again. He thought that he might have a prize on the line. But something started to go wrong. The fish was pulling ever stronger against Dino's grasp. Somehow it felt different than when he was holding the rod on the fishing vessel.

The dinghy started to drift away from the mother boat toward open water. Pulled back and forth by the prize catch, the boat was out of control. Mixed emotions instantly sent the angler into conflict. Common sense said to cut the line and release the catch. Reality said that letting go of the rod with one hand to reach for the hunting knife on his belt would mean that the rod and reel would instantly be gone with the fish. Ego said that he couldn't lose the equipment and, really, wouldn't it be great if he landed the monster.

Things progressively got worse. Each moment brought another challenge. How long could he hope to hold on? Dino rapidly epitomized that old saying of "*Not knowing if it was better to shit or go blind.*" Suddenly, it all ended! The boat lurched backward, the waters stilled and the silence was defining. Just as quickly as it had begun, the thrashing and tugging stopped dead...in the water—actually, really dead.

Dino's foolish attempt to fish from the dinghy came to Dr. Thomas Fogarty's attention. As he turned to get a better view, he saw it happen—a large shark struck the salmon on Dino's line and started to swallow it. Getting hooked, the shark started the violent fight to get free and also to keep his meal, resulting in Dino's wild ride.

Tom suddenly transformed from fisherman into hunter, his instincts immediately taking over. He asked for a rifle from one of the crew. (All fishing vessels carry arms to subdue bigger fish before bringing them on board.) Tom waited until the shark surfaced then dispatched it with a single shot. No sense wasting ammunition.

Dino, in contrast, never realized that his prize catch was just bait for the shark. He actually thought that he was fighting a big salmon. It was difficult to become a seasoned fisherman in one day. When the excitement was over Dino was instructed to cut off the carnage and row back to the boat. The disappointment of not being able to keep his trophy was overshadowed by the sheer stupidity of his fishing proficiency. Better to stick with medical research.

RACING FOR LIFE...THE REST OF THE STORY

SERENDIPITY, call it good luck, dumb luck, happenstance, a fluke, a lucky break, or just plain stumbling upon something when least expected. Fortunately or unfortunately, as the case may be, it is often at the heart (pun intended) of a donor/recipient story.

$\mathcal{A}$nticipation and bittersweet feelings prevailed at Cousin Lil Jim's house that Saturday night in September of 1968. Dino and his family were preparing to leave for a year in London. Family and friends were celebrating his assignment to the prestigious Hospital for Sick Children. The ladies were commiserating with his wife Betty, envisioning her hands full in moving to a strange location with two cute toddlers and an infant in tow. In the midst of the merrymaking, the phone rang. "It's for you, Dino. It's Dr. Cooley."

"Sorry, but I have to leave *right now*!" he said as he put down the phone. "All I know is that a baby born this afternoon in Evanston has to be immediately transported to Texas for a heart transplant. Dr. Cooley asked me to personally escort the infant to Houston and make sure it is kept alive until we get there." A taxi came to take him to Evanston Hospital, leaving the surprised guests as much in the dark as Dino.

Entering the Maternity ward, Dino was escorted to an anencephalic baby boy lying in an incubator. The head nurse told him that he was expected and that the paper work was ready to be signed. A heated ambulance was on call to take him to the airport. Looking at the papers Dino noted that the destination for the child was New York. "Must be a mistake, I'm taking this baby to St. Luke's Hospital in Houston, Texas; they are waiting for him there." A call to St. Luke's was made. Dr. Cooley's resident, Robert Bloodwell, verified that they were the designated receivers of the child. New York was crossed off and replaced with Texas, where a transplant recipient was waiting; they were on their way.

The unfortunate baby had been born without a developed brain. It was uncertain how long it could survive, but probably no longer than a day or two. Dino had to make sure the child was warm and kept alive until they could get to the hospital. Since no Air Ambulance flight was available at such short notice, the flight was made by a commercial carrier. They flew first class, with the pilot instructed to keep the plane temperature elevated and not to permit any smoking. (Remember those smoke filled cabins?). The other passengers were not very happy with the arrangements.

Dr. Bloodwell was waiting for them at the Houston airport. A quick trip to the hospital and the baby was soon safely in another incubator in the St. Like's maternity ward.

Transplant surgery, still new, was scheduled early that

morning. Dr. Cooley had performed ten transplants prior to this one, and seven were still alive. Unfortunately, after all that effort, the blood and tissue types were incompatible and the surgery was canceled. The infant was kept alive a few more days, but no compatible recipient was ever found.

Because of the cancelation the doctors had a chance to relax. Dino inquired as to what that New York stuff was all about? Dr. Cooley explained; he had been in New York the previous evening having dinner with Dr. Adrian Kantrowitz, a pioneer transplant surgeon from Brooklyn. They had been attending a meeting of the International Congress of the Transplant Society in New York. Dr. Kantrowitz mentioned that an anencephalic baby was available in Evanston, Illinois. Arrangements to bring the baby to New York fell through because the recipient child had died. Yet the baby was still there, and they were looking to find another recipient for that donor.

Dr. Cooley excused himself and ran for a telephone. He knew that a child was waiting for a donor heart back home. Getting his resident on the phone, he instructed Dr. Bloodwell to get that baby down to Texas right away before anyone else knew it was available. Back to the dinner, he again excused himself to get back home for an emergency. Nothing more was volunteered.

"Why did you call me?" Dino asked.

"Because I knew you could pull it off" was the reply. "Which reminds me, I also heard that DeBakey has a brain dead donor across the street in Methodist Hospital. They are keeping him alive until they find a recipient. I had his chart checked. He is a perfect donor for a man we have waiting here in St. Luke's. Let's go get him. I know we can pull this one off." (Transplant laws were not yet defined and, more importantly, there was a fierce competition between Dr. DeBakey and Dr. Cooley at that time.)

Dr. Cooley led the way with Dino and Dr. Bloodwell right behind him. They crossed the street, entered

Methodist Hospital and proceeded to the cardiovascular department. Stopping at the nurse's station, Dr. Cooley inquired, "Is Mike around?" (DeBakey hatred to be called Mike.)

"No, don't know where he is."

"We're here to transfer a patient across the street."

"But Dr. DeBakey has instructed us that no one is to leave this department without his permission."

"Well then, get him on the phone and check this out."

With that, Cooley ran to the room with the brain dead patient and had the two others assist him in disconnecting the man, then wheeling him, bed and all, IV in tow, down the hall towards the elevators. "Wait, I haven't heard from Dr. DeBakey yet!"

"Just tell him we couldn't wait," said Cooley as the elevator door closed.

Later that afternoon, after the completion of a successful transplant, Dr. Bloodwell asked, "What should we do with the bed?"

"We'll keep it here as a souvenir", said Dr. Cooley, and there it stayed for many years as a trophy in the Cooley/DeBakey war.

CLOUT! (With a Musical Refrain)

In order to survive you've got to know a guy who knows a guy. Chicago has been, and still is, a city that operates on the theory that it's not WHAT you know but WHO you know that counts.

The Hilton Hotel is located on the west side of beautiful Michigan Avenue, directly across the street from Grant Park. Doctors arriving for the annual meeting of the American College of Surgeons held at the hotel in the summer of 1981 could have looked out their windows and seen the bandstand. That was the furthest thing from their minds, although it would obliquely have a bearing on that gathering. The world renowned heart surgeons were there to meet their peers, learn from each other and, of course, have some fun relaxing away from the stress of the operating room.

The James C. Petrillo bandstand in Chicago's Grant Park stands as a monument to the little Italian trumpet player from the south side of the city that revolutionized the music industry in America. He joined ranks with the likes of Jimmy Hoffa, George Meany, John L. Lewis and other iron-fisted union leaders whose impact on the labor movement are felt even today.

Banquets are normally the concluding event of a convention and usually anticlimactic. Not so that year. A few doctors from Texas had been practicing with their musical group The Heartbeats, and were scheduled to perform at the banquet as a special treat. Where else could you have seen Drs. Denton Cooley, away from his Texas Heart Institute, playing the string bass, his associate, Ted Diethrich blowing trumpet, Dr. Grady Hallman (Director) sliding the trombone accompanied by another half dozen medical musicians.

Preparing for the banquet, the convention chairman asked that the hotel crew set up for the musicians. "What group will be playing?" asked the crew chief.

"The doctors," he replied.

"How many, and are they members of the Musician's union?"

"Of course not, they are practicing physicians."

"Sorry then, but they cannot perform here. According to union rules, this room is designated as a 12-member minimum venue, and only current card-carrying musician's union members can perform."

Meekly, the unbelieving chairman asked again, "Is there anything that we can do about this so that they can perform?"

"Not a chance in hell," said the fellow union brother with a knowing grin. "Remember, this is a labor town."

Shocked and befuddled, the convention chairman had just seen his program blown to pieces. What could he do to replace such an august group? How much misery would he be subjected to for having the doctors lug their instruments all the way to Chicago and then not being able to use them? Lack of thorough planning, derision, all of the above and more, were sure to fall upon him. He had no choice but to pass on the bad news to the soon-to-be-disgruntled Heartbeats.

Having a drink at the bar, a disappointed Dr. Diethrich lamented to Dino, "We can't play tonight because of some stupid union rule, and I'm really pissed!" Slowly digesting the news, Dino thought for a moment or two and said, "Excuse me, Ted; I just remembered something I must do. See you later." And with that he rushed out of the cocktail lounge leaving the rest of the musicians there to join Ted in his anger.

About a half hour had passed when the harried but relieved chairman returned to announce to the Heartbeats members: "It's okay to practice. You are now allowed to perform this evening." He didn't know how or why the situation had changed, he said, but the hotel manager had contacted him a few minutes ago to tell him that the doctors could go on with the show.

Dino had remembered that our aunt Gertie's brother, Nick Bliss just happened to be the president of the Chicago Musicians Union at that time. "I'll give him a call and explain the situation, Dino thought, and perhaps he can find a way to help us out."

Nick understood the dilemma and was only too happy to assist. He *found* a clause in the contract that provided for *special performances*. A call to the hotel was all it took to straighten things out. "By the way, Dino, there has to be a union musician present during the performance. He doesn't have to play but must be there to observe. Since I haven't seen you for a while, I think that I'll come over and join you for a drink while they play... I've got to admit that I'm kind of curious to see how well these great doctors operate as musicians." (They were actually exceptionally good.)

Few people realized that evening just how close they came to missing the doctors' musical entertainment. Dino remembered something we had been taught by our dad as kids: *A good deed is something to be accomplished without acknowledgement or fanfare.* But Dino also knew that, when needed, using a little bit of *clout* never hurts.

Incidentally, retired Dr. Grady L. Hallman continued his love of music and eventually played with the Dallas Symphony Orchestra, as a card-carrying musician's union member.

EXPENDABLE

They were "expendable". Society abused them. Nobody cared for them, they were left to die. Grave diggers buried them. Charles Dickens immortalized them.

London experienced exponential growth with the end of the Napoleonic wars, the Industrial Revolution, and gentrification. The ensuing population explosion also brought with it disease, and famine, disproportionately affecting children. In 1843, fifty-one thousand people died in London; almost half were children. A survey revealed that there were some 2,400 patients in various London hospitals, but only 26 were children under 10 years of age. With little healthcare available for children, and little hope of survival even if they were attended to, the sick children were generally considered "expendable," and left to die in the arms of their grieving mothers.

Dr. Charles West was trained in France and Germany, where he studied gynecology and pediatrics. Childcare facilities existed at that time in both of those countries. Upon returning to Britain he was struck with the lack of any meaningful facility specifically catering to children's needs. He soon undertook the challenge of creating a hospital devoted to the care and treatment of children. With the backing of philanthropists, West succeeded. In 1852 he purchased a hundred-year-old mansion at No. 49, Great Ormond Street, in a teeming slum district of London. The hospital located there initially opened with a pair of ten-bed wards, one for boys and one for girls.

Limited medical knowledge at the time restricted treatment to minor ailments and infectious diseases. Clean conditions, proper nutrition and loving care there may have benefited the patient more than prevailing medicine. Surgery was still questionable. Sterilization was something new. Anesthesia and x-rays didn't exist until the early 1900s. Few doctors were trained to cut into the body. The main talent of the surgeon of the day was to limit the patient's suffering before he passed out.

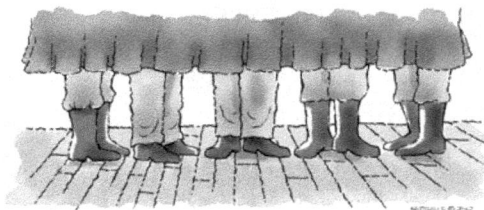

By the end of the century medicine was rapidly improving, primarily due to myriad important techniques and discoveries coming on line. In 1877, Joseph Lister, a British surgeon, pioneered antiseptic surgery with the use of carbolic acid. Eventually, the operating suites in the hospital all had tile walls and floors. A carbolic acid "Mist Generator" spewed moist vapor into the air. As a result, everything in the operating suite became damp. A floor drain was usually located in the center of the room, beneath the operating table, to dispose of the condensing moisture. Ether and chloroform were introduced as anesthetics, initiating the advent of painless surgery. Pharmaceuticals supplanted historic home remedies. In 1903, after the Curies discovered x-rays, the hospital acquired its first machine capable of peering inside the body. As each new step developed, the hospital on Great Ormond Street kept up with changing medical practice by continually opening additional specialty departments.

Jumping ahead, in 1926 Sir Dennis Browne, the first surgeon to work exclusively on children, developed treatments in neonatal and orthopedic abnormalities. By the end of World War II in 1945, advancements in treating wounded soldiers led to the opening of specialties in plastic and neurosurgery. It wasn't until 1955, however, that a cardiac unit was opened.

Cardiac surgery was just evolving in the 1950s, and never before had been attempted on hearts the size of walnuts. The cardiothoracic unit opened under the guidance and direction of Mr. David Waterston, a surgeon, (differentiated from physicians and designated "Mr." in Britain) and cardiologist Dr. Richard Bonham Carter. They pioneered open heart procedures for corrective surgery on newborns. The Hospital for Sick Children on Great Ormond Street was always a teaching as well as a research institution. World renowned, it draws the best of the best to seek acceptance for training there. While working at the National Institutes of Health, National Heart Institute, Dr. Constantine "Dino" Tatooles was made aware of Great Ormond Street and the great work of Mr. Waterston and his staff. He was encouraged to apply as a senior registrar (resident) should the opportunity ever present itself.

Dino completed his two-year tour of duty working at

the National Heart Institute in Bethesda, MD and then returned to the University of Chicago Hospital in 1966 as a Senior Resident. As fate would have it, he returned for a visit to NHI in 1967, while Mr. Eoin Aberdeen, the assistant chief of surgery under Mr. Waterston, was there for a visit. After introductions, Dino boldly asked Mr. Aberdeen if there was a chance that he could go to London and train under Mr. Waterston. Dr. Glen Morrow, head of the clinic of surgery at NHI, and Dino's former professor, picked up on the conversation and enthusiastically told Aberdeen that Dino was a perfect candidate for their cardiac unit. There was not a comparable facility in the States where a doctor could receive such intensive pediatric cardiac training. A few months later, back in Chicago, Dino received a letter from Mr. Waterston offering the opportunity to train with him at Great Ormond Street in the 1968 class. That year Dino, his wife and three small children were on a plane headed for London.

He reported for duty at Great Ormond Street on a Friday afternoon. Dr. Michael Tynan, a cardiologist, along with Dr. Jaroslav Stark, a surgeon, took Dino on the customary tour of the institution. Mr. Waterston, however, was not available and remained a mystery man. Mr. Aberdeen, who had had previously advised Dino that there probably would be no opportunity for him to go "hands on" in surgery for at least a month or two, was also missing. Dr. Tynan amended that thought when he told Dino, "By the way, old chap, you are now officially on duty this weekend." After a trip to the doctors' locker room and a change into clean scrubs, he was left on his own.

Several hours later a newborn "blue baby" barely an hour old was admitted through the emergency room and brought into the operating suite. The baby needed a Waterston shunt to be installed. This was a temporary fix that Mr. Waterston had pioneered which connected the aorta directly to the pulmonary artery for a year or two until the child could become strong enough for a permanent correction.

Seeking direction, Dino called Mr. Waterston. Waterston instructed Dino to prepare for surgery and to meet him in the operating suite ready to make the fix. Passing through the locker room, Dino had noticed rows of funny boots lined up against the wall. "Lister Boots" he was told. They were needed when standing on the damp operating room floor. He put on a pair, scrubbed, and entered the operating room. The anesthesiologist was ready to proceed. A young junior registrar was also there waiting to assist. As Dino stepped up to the operating table with the newborn draped for the operation, Mr. Waterston shuffled into the room. He looked at Dino for the first time and asked, "Do you know what you are doing?" Dino replied "yes sir". Mr. Waterston waited a second, and with a nod said, "Well then, carry on", and left the room. The next time they met was at 9:00 am the next morning in the nursery looking down on a baby recovering nicely from the previous night's operation. Thus began the start of a wonderful friendship.

No longer was a child, even a newborn with serious heart deformities, ever expendable.

ROSES

Divulged trade secrets and unintended results of their misapplication...

*I*n 1455, the Royal House of Lancaster (whose emblem was a red rose) went to war with the Royal House of York (whose emblem was a white rose). The conflict between the two rival branches of the royal house of Plantagenet ended in 1485. Historians have called this period "The Wars of the Roses". Henry the VII of Lancaster eventually married Elizabeth of York to unite and reconcile the two houses. Since that period, the national flower and emblem of England has been the rose.

For Englishmen, growing a prizewinning rose garden is a coveted achievement. Topping even that accomplishment is having one's hybrid rose "named" for its distinct and unique beauty. Mr. David James Waterston, CBE, MBE, FRCS, achieved that distinction several times, as his rose garden won awards year after year. (Note: in England physicians are referred to as "Doctor" but surgeons are distinctively called "Mister". Nurses are customarily referred to as "Sister".)

Many believed he cherished his gardening skills more than the brilliant surgery he performed day after day at the Hospital for Sick Children on Great Ormond Street in London. As most Brits often do, Waterston also enjoyed an occasional pint or two with friends in his favorite neighborhood pub.

One Sunday afternoon, while in the pub on a break from his gardening chores, a messenger raced in to find Mr. Waterston and inform him that he was urgently needed at the hospital. Unbeknownst to him, a call had been made to Ormond Street for the best surgeon on staff. Simultaneously, instructions were relayed to vacate the seventh floor of the hospital for an inbound patient. A wing of the floor was cleared and security was posted. Meanwhile, down in the main administrative section of the hospital, in the ornately paneled board room, there was a rapidly convening group of members of the Royal College of Surgeons and Physicians.

The British National Health System regulations contain a provision that permission is not required to perform surgery on a patient, if in the opinion of the attending physician, immediate intervention is required. Such was the case with the emergency at hand. Upon entering the hospital, Mr. Waterston was escorted to the patient and made a quick observation that a "hot" appendix was the problem. He immediately had the patient sent down to the operating suite.

Meanwhile, the board room filled with members of the royal court joining an increasing army of royal physicians. All anxiously awaited a diagnosis and suggested treatment for the special patient. A consultation with the royal family and assembled advisors was to ensure that proper care would be administered.

After a seemingly interminable wait, a hospital staff member entered the boardroom with a crumpled envelope in hand. Delivered promptly to the awaiting Queen Elizabeth, the scribbled note on the back read *"The Prince of Wales had an inflamed appendix and I performed an appendectomy I shall see him at 9:00 am tomorrow morning."* The Queen, the Prince's mother, asked to see Mr. Waterston. She was informed that he had just left the hospital for home, to finish attending to his roses.

Traditionally, physicians attending royalty receive the Knighthood designation of "Sir" for their service. Mr. Waterston, not a particularly enthusiastic fan of the monarchy, had to wait a year before he was designated an "M.B.E." (Member of the British Empire), a distinct honor, to be sure, but a step below being called "Sir". It did not faze him a bit, since his roses truly were more important to him than a mere title.

Shortly after that incident, Mr. Waterston invited his new senior surgical registrar and wife out to the Waterston country estate for a visit and dinner. Dr. Constantine J. (Dino) Tatooles, accompanied by his wife Betty and their three toddlers, had just arrived from America for a year's assignment working in the pediatric cardiac surgery unit headed by Mr. Waterston. The compulsory tour of the estate and, of course, the rose gardens, had been conducted numerous times throughout the years. To the English guests this was customary for a proper country manor. To the Tatooles', however, the grounds, and especially the rose garden, were like nothing they had seen before.

As time passed Dino and David Waterston became close friends in addition to medical associates. Waterston gradually took the young registrar into his confidence. He told him, for instance, that during the period of treating the young royal he never called him Charles or the Prince of Wales. He always referred to him as "Charlie", and rather than having to bow down to the Queen after performing the appendectomy, he just left for home to tend to his roses.

Speaking of those prizewinning roses, one day Mr. Waterston divulged to Dino his deepest and most importantly kept secret. In the early pioneering days of open heart surgery the heart lung machines depended on fresh blood to function. (Today special serums are used instead of blood.) Several units of blood that matched the patient's blood-type had to be collected and kept on hand to permit the pump to function during the procedure. At the conclusion of the operation the blood was removed and disposed of prior to sterilizing the machine and preparing to refill it with fresh blood for the next procedure. Mr. Waterston knew there was no better nutrient-filled fertilizer for his roses than the used blood, so he diligently collected all the expended blood, took it home and used it to fertilize his rose gardens. No one else in all of England had access to this superior plant food.

After the year was up, Dino and his family returned home to America to a new house that his brother Jim, a contractor, had built for him during his absence. Dino returned to the University of Chicago Medical Center, where he performed his newly acquired skills of pediatric heart surgery. The home was not yet landscaped. Since Dino was now totally immersed in his new position at the hospital, he had little time to tend to completion of the house. His wife Betty took on the added responsibility of getting readjusted stateside in a new house that needed decorating, getting the kids comfortably enrolled in school, and day to day maintenance. She also was charged with seeing that proper landscaping surrounded their new abode. Dino's only request was that it must include a sizeable rose garden. Remembering Mr. Waterston's estate, Betty concurred; not only would it be a great idea but it would also be a fond memento of their year abroad in England.

Several months later Betty complained that flies were constantly buzzing around their beautiful rose patch. The gardeners had no explanation. One night Dino arrived late from the hospital and instead of going directly into the house, he first paid a visit to the rose garden. Betty noticed him through the kitchen window and saw Dino pouring something from a plastic container around the flowers. Words were exchanged; a long-kept secret was revealed. Shortly thereafter, along with the Wars of the Roses, the garden also was history.

"WHERE ARE YOU?"

Quite often a person has to become completely and utterly lost before ever hoping to have a chance of really finding himself. The return trip can be very enlightening.

*"H*e looked just like Tony."

"Yes, but where are you?"

Dino had returned to America after serving a year performing pediatric heart surgery at the Hospital for Sick Children on Great Ormond Street in London, England. He joined the staff of Loyola University Medical Center as the Assistant Chief of Cardiac Surgery at the newly completed hospital in Maywood, Illinois. A mile away I had recently completed building a midrise office building. The proximity of my new office there afforded us the opportunity of occasionally meeting for a drink after work and catching up on a year's absence.

Such was the case one afternoon when I tried to no avail to reach him. Gone from the hospital, I tried calling Dino on his mobile phone, a privilege extended to just a few at that time. Messages were left unanswered. As I was leaving the office the phone finally rang. It was Dino. "Where are you?" I asked. A distraught voice answered, "I don't know or care; I have to get away to clear my head." He kept repeating, "He looked just like Tony." I persisted. "Can we meet somewhere?" "Not tonight" was the troubled reply, "we can talk later." It took a few more days before I could get to the bottom of that uncomfortable moment.

A three-year-old child born with Hypo plastic Left Heart Syndrome (HLHS) lay ill in a nearby hospital. Word that a pediatric cardiothoracic surgeon recently joined the staff at the Loyola Medical Center precipitated a transfer of the child to the new facility. Dino met with the parents, examined the patient and reconfirmed the previous diagnosis; unfortunately, HLHS is a congenital heart defect that was non-operative at that time with little or no hope of survival.

In normal births a healthy heart is formed to receive oxygen rich blood from the lungs, which is then pumped out to nourish the body. In an HLHS child the aorta and left ventricle are undeveloped at birth, thus preventing sufficient amounts of blood to flow. Without intervention HLHS is fatal. Palliative care procedures have since been developed to offer relief, but the only true cure available at present is a heart transplant. Even today fifty percent of HLHS patients, usually with other complications, are still treated with "compassionate care" instead of surgery.

For three days the mother pleaded with Dr. Tatooles. *Please, please* try ANYTHING! There must be something possible to save my baby. When Dino first examined the child he was struck with the realization that it looked just like his three-year-old son, Tony. A real or subconscious kinship developed. What could he do to save this child? As a pioneering high risk surgeon, he had to look at all alternatives.

Blue baby operations were routine procedures when he worked in London. Alterations were made to the defective heart to provide relief and hope of an extended lifetime. At that time, however, they were not taking any HLHS cases. Dino gave much thought to the situation. Building on his previous training, what if he could devise a way for oxygenated blood to be rerouted through the heart? To his knowledge this had not yet been accomplished. After two days of concentrated thought, a plan was devised whereby temporary corrections could be made. That would afford time for more corrective work at a later date. The question remained, was the heart conformed in such a way to accommodate the renovation and strong enough survive the surgery?

The parents were consulted and a possible solution was discussed. It was repeatedly stressed to them that it was experimental, never performed before and had a very high risk of their child not surviving the operation. Even if he did survive, he would face a life of additional surgery and never function as a normal child. Dino estimated the risk at 90% -10%, and advised against it. But the mother was adamant: do everything you can to try to save my baby, and hang the risk. The operation was scheduled for the following morning.

Dino looked at the child on the operating table. The subconscious thought that he looked like Tony was erased from his mind, and he went to work. Slowly and carefully the heart was exposed. The defects became visible and it was obvious as to why the little heart didn't work properly. Dino's solution was viable. He performed the reconstruction, closed the operation and waited. At first it appeared that all had gone well. Unfortunately, the malformed configuration of the heart would not permit enough blood to flow through the reconstructed area, and the child died. Dino was devastated.

Sitting in the doctor's room, Dino struggled through a cup of coffee, held his head in his hands and cried. He dreaded meeting the parents who were anxiously waiting for him outside the door in the hallway. Dino could not mention the word "baby". "The heart died," he said to them.

"YOU KILLED MY BABY!" The mother was frantic, explosive, and beyond tears. "YOU KILLED MY BABY!" she screamed over and over again as she pounded on Dino's chest. The distraught mother's lament could be heard throughout the tiled hallways of the building. Dino kept thinking that the baby looked like Tony and never felt the flaying.

He dressed in a daze, went to his car and drove off to who knows where. He had to get away to clear his head. Some hours later Dino came home. Without a word he went into the bedroom of his sleeping three-year-old Tony. He couldn't stop hugging and kissing him.

In 1978, at a meeting concerning surgical repairs of pediatric cardiac congenital anomalies, Dr. Francis Fontan of the University of Bordeaux in France presented a paper on his tricuspid atresia procedure. Ironically, Dino was at that same meeting to present *his* paper on another congenital anomaly. The two doctors instantly related to each other because of their common interests and became close associates. Dino was invited to meet with Fontan at the University of Bordeaux, but never made it there. Fontan, however, did come to operate with Dino in America. Years later, Dino's son Tony did make the trip to France. He spent a summer there training as a medical resident under Dr. Fontan working on congenital heart defects.

Many things materialized as a result of that episode. Dino never operated on a *person* again. Henceforth, he only operated on *hearts*. To this day Dino cannot remember patients' faces, but he never forgets what their hearts looked like. That event took place in 1969. The definitive procedure for HLHS was devised by Dr. Norwood in 1981, in conjunction with variations of the Fontan procedure. Dino first came up with his ideas in 1969, fully twelve years ahead of the others.

CIRCUIT De MONACO

So many races...auto races, track races, election races, foot races; none, however can be more meaningful than the race to save a life.

The Lowes (hotel) hairpin turn is so tight that drivers gear down to twenty-nine mph so as not to spin out. Through the next two turns, Formula 1 racers get back to speeds of 160 mph. Originated in 1929, the Grand Prix de Monaco is one of the racing treasures of the world. Living the sights, sounds and the beautiful surroundings of the track twisting about the streets of Monaco is a unique experience to behold.

In 1971, Dr. Edward D. "Ted" Diethrich created the Arizona Heart Institute in Phoenix. Open heart surgery, then in its infancy, was still perceived as extremely high risk. In those exciting early days of cardiovascular surgery, Dr. Dierthrich wanted to bring the latest procedures he helped to develop at the Texas Heart Institute while working under the tutelage of Dr. Denton Cooley to needy patients in the Southwest. Because of Dr. Diethrich's reputation, people in need sought him out and followed him to his new facility.

Shortly after it opened, Dino flew to Phoenix to see his friend Ted and his new Institute. During his visit a prominent executive in the gaming and entertainment field was admitted for an open heart procedure. Ted invited Dino to scrub in and observe the institute team in action. The operation was successful. Greatly relieved, the grateful gentleman couldn't stop thanking Dr. Diethrich, and his fellow surgeon friend, Dino, for giving invalids like himself a new lease on life with their surgical skills.

Sometime later, Dr. Diethrich received a call from the newly reinvigorated fellow. "Every year I take a few of my friends to Monte Carlo to see the Grand Prix race. This year I would like you to join us and, by the way, bring your friend Dino with you." After some back and forth discussions, the call ended with an insistence that they both come as his honored guests.

The accommodations at the Lowes Grand (now the Fairmont) were not only plush; they afforded the best spot in town to view the race. Sharing the experience with some of the host's other guests, the long weekend event was enjoyable, memorable and strangely fulfilling.

Preparations for the race begin months in advance to create the in-city raceway. The city is literally brought to a standstill during race weekend. As a compromise to the gentry, accommodations are made in the schedule to keep some semblance of commerce functioning. On Thursdays there are practice runs, Friday the barricades are temporarily moved; no racing scheduled to allow the city to briefly return to normal. On Saturday, time trials determine the winner of the pole position, and finally, Sunday is the day of the seventy-eight lap racing spectacle.

The trip over to France was unique in itself. The host had arranged for his American guests to fly from New York to Paris aboard the Supersonic Transport jetliner, (no longer in commission) hitting speeds of over Mach 1.5. A private chartered jet took them to Nice. Thursday was spent settling in, meeting the other guests at the party, watching the time trials, drinks, dinner and not unexpectedly, everyone ending the evening in the world famous casino.

Dr. Dierthrich had an interest in the America's Cup race and had heard of a sail maker in nearby Nice who specialized in big boat riggings. He had discussed this with Dino and on a non-racing day, Friday, they took off to find the boat shop. Ted brought white jackets from the Arizona Heart Institute with his and Dino's names embroidered on them. They both wore white pants, shirts and shoes. To complete the ensemble, they rented two white Kawasaki sport bikes for the trip to Nice. Except for the white biker helmets, they might have looked like Good Humor Ice Cream vendors.

The trip to locate the sail maker's shop entailed biking through a myriad of unfamiliar side streets. As they continued the quest, the screaming voice of a distraught person was heard ahead. Slowing to investigate, they came upon a sobbing woman half holding and half dragging a very young child down the street. She was apparently making her way toward a pharmacy on the corner ahead. Stopping and dismounting their bikes, the two men in white ran to the lady, took the child from her arms and brought it into the "drug store."

It became immediately evident that the little boy was in cardiac arrest. Dino lifted the child, swung it upside down and proceeded to thump it soundly on the back. Food particles were expelled, but the child did not resume breathing. Dr. Diethrich laid the child on the floor of the store and proceeded to administer CPR. In the meantime, the store jammed with bystanders. So many people amassed that the sidewalk outside was overflowing with curiosity seekers. Shortly, a French EMT team arrived and worked their way into the crowded pharmacy. Dressed totally in black, they were a sharp contrast to the white-garbed doctors working over the child on the floor.

Unfortunately, the EMT team did not have any equipment small enough to use on a child. The two doctors had no alternative but to keep pumping the little boy's chest. Thankfully, after about twenty-five minutes, the child began to breath and started to cry. The EMTs gently placed the infant on a gurney and, along with the distraught mother, drove off in their vehicle with lights flashing and that European wee-woo, wee-woo siren blaring.

Dino and Ted got up, brushed themselves off and proceeded out of the store through a gauntlet opened by the still loitering onlookers. Once outside, as they made their way to the bikes, the crowd erupted into cheers and clapping. The two white knights put on their helmets, started their Kawasakis and drove off down the street.

No one had ever bothered to ask them who they were or where they came from!

THE NEW NIKON

In a teaching institution the camera is often times as important as clamps, forceps or other medical devices. Prior to videos and digital photograph, 35mm slides were the normal visual aid used for teaching, giving lectures and at formal presentations.

Dino had an old worn out 35mm Pentax Cannon camera that had served him well, but it was time to replace it. After consultations with others, trips to the camera shop, soul searching and vacillation, he finally picked up the esteemed Nikon SLR from Helix Cameras downtown store and brought it to his office at the University of Chicago. But opportunities to put the new camera to use just didn't seem to materialize. Pictures were taken of his staff, the beautiful gothic campus and even dogs in the lab, but sill there was nothing happening to merit use of his new "toy". Patience, something was bound to turn up to merit the use of this fine instrument.

Then as now, weekends in the south side of Chicago were unfortunately rife with rival gang members fighting for turf. Some of the most violent of these fights occurred in the neighborhoods surrounding and adjacent to the hospital. This guaranteed that at least a dozen or more members would end up to the emergency room of the hospital with stab wounds, shootings and even DOAs.

On one particularly hot summer Saturday evening, the strong-willed leader of one of the most notorious gangs was brought in with a wound to the chest. Because of his prominence, a large entourage followed him into the emergency room. They were disruptive and chanting to no one in particular, "If he dies, you all die!"

Dino was called to the ER to stabilize the well-known leader and bring him to the operating suite. A huge, particularly menacing lieutenant came up to Dino, pushed his finger into the doctor's chest and repeated, "If he dies, you die." Dino stared intently into the face of the big fellow with a sneer and a grin. "What are you looking at?" the surprised fellow asked. "I just want to be sure that I can remember you," Dino replied, "because if you come in here next week, my fingers just might slip while working on you."

"No, doc, I was only kidding", the suddenly docile lieutenant replied. "Please doc, help my friend." "Well then", Dino said "get these bums out of here so we can do our job." And with that, the room emptied.

Once in the operating room the prominent patient was prepared for surgery. Dino scrubbed, checked with the attending crew, and then opened the chest to find the source of the bleeding. It soon became obvious that the patient had been hit with a piercing shot that had made a small hole in the wall of his heart. Upon observing the situation, Dino turned away and shouted, "Quick, get my camera!" He then stopped the leaking wound by placing one of his fingers into the hole in the heart.

One of the attending interns came back in with the

virgin Nikon in hand. Dino positioned the fellow on his side, slightly beside him. "Aim across the table toward the overhead operating room light," he said. "Shoot when I tell you."

Dino was well aware of the strong beat of the heart in his hand. He could feel the pressure build as the chamber with the now plugged hole filled with blood. "Get ready, SHOOT!" Timing it perfectly, Dino pulled his finger out of the small hole just as the pressure built up in the chamber. A fine spray of blood flew across the operating table highlighted by the overhead light shimmering behind it. Dino quickly reinserted his finger into the small hole.

The remainder of the operation proceeded as a routine repair. The hole was sutured, the exit wound closed and the patient, a strong, well-built individual, had a rapid recovery. Today that individual is still a dynamic leader. Long exited from the world of gangs, he now represents his people as a successful member of our government.

What about the picture? That also turned out well. For years a large surrealistic photograph hung on Dino's office wall. The blending of colors intertwining with the subdued light shining through the mist was something to behold. There never was a valid explanation of the abstract picture. The Nikon, also, did its job professionally, as expected.

"The Greeks"

Only in America, where the streets are paved in gold...

The original "Greeks" were two Greek immigrant brothers. Our uncles, Gus and Nick Maggos, left Greece in the early 1900s to find their fortune in America. Working their way up the ranks from dishwashers, bus boys, to cooks, they soon were operating a small snack shop in the old Illinois Central Station. In the mid-1920s (no one now recalls the exact date), the brothers moved their snack shop to a small store on Harrison Street across from Cook County Hospital.

Fortune visited them when Dr. Karl A. Meyer, the dynamic driving force of the hospital across the street, stopped in to check out his new neighbors. An immediate and dynamic lifetime connection formed between them and developed into something that surpassed all of their expectations.

At that time medical schools and nearby hospitals were dedicated to their respective tasks, and that did not include facilities for meals. Dr. Meyer, after thoroughly checking out the store, its owners and food, suggested to his medical staff that they might find the little snack shop across the street convenient for a fast meal. This accomplished several things for Dr. Meyer: first, the staff did not have to venture out of the area (he knew where they were when he needed them), and second, he was able to save money for the hospital by not having to relegate funds to build a food facility within the building. The little snack shop soon became an extension of the hospital. A telephone was eventually installed so that the hospital staff could reach the doctors when they were needed. The store was officially designated as "Ward 38."

Other workers at the hospital soon discovered the medical staff across the street and decided to join them. As they crowded into the small store a conflict arose as to who would occupy the space. Again, Dr. Meyer to the rescue! He convinced the brothers that they had to expand. As time went by, visitors to the hospital also started to stop in. They, however, had another purpose in mind. Besides taking carry-outs with them for the patients that they were visiting, they were also looking for other things to bring besides food.

During the period of the Second War, the nearby YMCA was taken over by the Army to house soldiers. Once more, the need arose to feed others. This prompted several more expansions, and finally motivated the brothers to buy the entire building. As a result, "*The Greeks*" became a dining and shopping oasis in the midst of a rapidly growing, medically-oriented neighborhood. Years later, as part of a beautification program, the buildings located across from Cook County Hospital were to be demolished to allow for the creation of a park. Because of a grandfathered contract between "*The Greeks*" and the hospital, instigated by Dr. Meyer, the building could remain standing as long as it contained the restaurant and was owned and operated by the Maggos Family.

The building had two entrances, the corner double door led through a vestibule into a forerunner of today's mini-mart. Upon entering, one passed by a long glass-fronted counter. Below the glass case was a vast assortment of cigars and cigarettes. On top, and next to the vestibule, was the chrome multi-buttoned cash register. It stood as a guard station with a family member always on duty to make sure that no one left without paying. Walking further into the space there was a display where flowers could be purchased to take across the street in order to cheer patients' rooms. If that did not appeal, then nearby were fruit bins with apples, oranges, bananas, as well as other choices. Of course, a large candy case was there as well. Finally, one could also find the typical souvenir dolls, trinkets and get well cards on display to make sure that anyone visiting patients would not go empty-handed. For those hungry workers from across the street there was a large serpentine counter and cafeteria at the rear portion of this large front area. The operation was open twenty-four hours, every day of the week, and no one can now remember if there ever was a key for the front door.

A single, nondescript side door led into quite another world. At the center of the building was a bar and a more formal dining facility. One could enter this area through the front door, but typically anyone that came into this section was considered family. The side door was considered to be the entrance to a semi-private club. That was where the doctors, nurses, medical detail salesmen, politicians and visiting dignitaries could be found. But, at the far end of the building, next to and through the lounge area, was an inner sanctum for those truly in favor—the infamous "Monkey Room". Painted murals on the walls featured jungle scenes of palm trees with swinging monkeys; hence, the name. If the front part of the store was a forerunner of the "mini mart", then the Monkey Room surely was a pattern for today's club scene. There was no bouncer at the entrance to the "club", but if there was not a nod of approval from one of the family members, it was all but impossible to gain entrance.

What was so special? Interns and Residents could sit one-on-one with their professors over a beer and gain more insight about medicine than they ever could have learned while making rounds or in a classroom. Distraught family members might be consoled there after the loss of a loved one. Nurses and doctors were introduced and later married as a result of meeting in the Monkey Room. And one cannot even begin to contemplate how many political arrangements were hatched at a corner table in that dimly lit smoke-filled room. (Remember, even doctors smoked then.) Medical detail salesmen were always good for a free drink, and wise doctors and staff knew how to play that game.

George Dunne, then the Commissioner of Cook County, and the titular head of the hospital, enjoyed stopping by for a meal and a drink or two. He often found "*The Greeks*" to be a first-hand source of hospital operations. As an example, the aftermath of having a conversation with Dr. Tatooles, then head of the Cardio-Thoracic Department, resulted in the construction of a eighth floor level skyway bridge. He heard of inefficiencies in their unit because the operating suites were located on the eighth floor, but in two separate buildings. One could look across the courtyard and wave to associates in the other building, but it was terribly inefficient to have to walk down from one section, cross to the other building, and then walk up again to the eighth floor on the other side. The interconnecting causeway saved valuable time and improved care for the patients.

The store was also a philanthropic haven for the many interns and residents that worked long hours and were barely able to exist on the money they earned; they were never refused a meal because of lack of funds. It was normal business to allow them to run up large tabs. Though many years might have passed, it was not unusual for a proud doctor to revisit his early guardian to make good on his tab. Many others that were struggling to keep on their medical path worked on the side as bus boys, waiters, and a few as bartenders. The untold story, however, remains as to how many of the future doctors had also received "silent" scholarships from the Maggos family. It numbered in the hundreds. Lore has it that not a bill or obligation ever went unpaid.

And speaking of family, the two immigrant brothers married well, had large families and saw some of their offspring become professionals. Fortunately, a few others kept the family tradition alive by working their way up the ranks within the store. The brothers never learned to drive, shared a two flat residence that was located near their church, and at the end of the Harrison streetcar line so that a car was unnecessary. Many hours were spent at the store but time was found for philanthropic endeavors at their beloved church. As time passed, and the now old and proud brothers went to their rewards, their children continued to run *The Greeks* in the same traditions started by their fathers.

Urban growth and eminent domain eventually put an end to that old institution, but ask around and you will be told that *The Greeks* surely is as much a part of Chicago's Medical History as is Cook County Hospital.

CONSCIENTIOUS—TO A FAULT

Lake effect snow is particular to the Great Lakes Region. It can shut down cities, please kids when schools close; and, in Chicago's case, even cause an obscure female politician, Jane Byrne, to become Mayor of Chicago as a result of the January, 1979 storm. Natives ingeniously have learned to cope and even take advantage of the situation.

Saint Joseph Hospital is located off Lake Shore Drive, across the park from Lake Michigan. An unobstructed path of wind-borne snow blowing across the lake ends at the front door of the hospital. Even a light snowfall is magnified in intensity because of the hospital's location.

Dino was on the staff of the hospital in the winter of 1979, the year of the big "Jane Byrne" storm. For some inexplicable reason, Dino became overly concerned that the potential of heavy snow would prevent him from getting to St. Joe. More likely, though, that was only a justification for him to purchase a new four-wheel-drive Chevy Blazer. In his typical style, Dino had every conceivable option available installed on the vehicle. Weeks passed, and Chicago was experiencing one of its mildest winters. No chances to test or prove the reason for his purchase. He was mercilessly teased that the Blazer certainly was not the car for him, but more appropriate for one of his children.

After an unusually warm week in January, a few snowflakes began to appear. Then more and more appeared. The winds picked up and didn't stop. After two days the city was blanketed with eighteen inches of heavy wet snow. The Sanitation Department was caught completely off guard. The city streets were slow to be cleared. Chicago was frozen solid and came to a standstill. That unprepared department and the resulting turmoil cost Mayor Bilandic his job.

And Dino was vindicated. His Blazer performed as promised and brought him to work at the snowbound hospital. Unwilling to take any unnecessary chances, he wisely stayed at the hospital overnight. With many of the staff not able to make it to work, those that were there couldn't leave and soon were overburdened. After two days of non-strop effort, Dino had an idea to reward some of his associates and interns...

The Tango restaurant was located in the Belmont Hotel, about a mile away from the hospital. Doctors often frequented it for dinner or after work relaxation. "Let's take a break and all go to the Tango for a late dinner," Dino suggested. "My Blazer should make it there with no sweat." An appreciative group of tired doctors followed Dino down to the garage.

The streets were eerily empty on the trip to the restaurant. When they pulled up to the door a cheerful fellow appeared at the curbside walkway. "I'll take your car," he said, and gave Dino a ticket stub in exchange for the keys. Dino always had the car parked by the valet because vacant spaces were never available near the typically busy intersection where the hotel was located. The group raced into the restaurant to get out of the cold.

It was a relaxing and deserved break but all too soon the trip back to the hospital could not be prolonged. Bills paid, heavy coats and scarves put on, the group proceeded back to the car. Dino looked but could not see the valet. He walked back to the manager and asked, "Where is the car hiker?"

"Sorry Dino", he replied, "since the snow storm no one has been driving and we didn't need him."

So much for that Blazer; the skeleton of a once proud automobile was found stripped in a vacant lot on the south side of Chicago. The replacement vehicle did not have the oversize tires, chrome wheels and other sundry accessories. And, as previously touted, after the winter storms had passed, so the Blazer was passed...on to his kids.

The insurance company was glad that Dino still had the stub to substantiate his claim.

CHAMPIONSHIP RING

The thrill of the elusive victory, the athlete winning; is that not the same as the quest of the hunter, or for that matter the doctor's completion of his operation. Challenges, competition, desire, training, ultimately instinct, and the rush of success unite them all as one.

*I*n 1934, the then Mayor of Chicago, Edward J. Kelly, initiated the City of Chicago Prep Bowl. Public and Catholic High School League champions played in Soldier Field on the Friday after Thanksgiving as a fundraiser to help needy children. Immensely popular, in 1937 one hundred and twenty-five thousand fans came to watch setting an all-time amateur sporting event attendance record. Dino played in Soldier Field on the 1953 St. George team that beat Austin High 38-12.

College ball came to an abrupt end with a debilitating knee injury. Sports, however, and football in particular, would not go away. Years later the itch had to be scratched. Dr. Ted Diethrich helped to form the USFL and bought an interest in the Chicago Blitz. That short-lived venture sparked Dino to also get involved. He sponsored the River Grove Cowboys, a local semi-professional team. He had the good fortune of having Doug Buffone, the record-holding linebacker for the Chicago Bears, as his manager. (Years later, Doug and Dino would help to form the new Arena Football League.)

Aspiring athletes play in the semi-pro leagues. By training and keeping in shape they hope to be scouted into the big time. The Cowboys were fortunate to have such a handful of young hopefuls on the team in 1987. Their desires, along with excellent coaching, helped to mold the team. They were sharp, focused and finished the season as champions of the Midwest League. At the victory dinner, large gilded championship rings were presented to all.

Dino was pleased with the team's accomplishment. He kept the ring in his pocket and took it out for all to see. When the story lost its appeal, the ring ultimately found a resting place in Dino's desk at the hospital. One evening, while preparing to leave, he spotted the ring in the drawer. Probably better that I bring it home, he thought, and with that he absentmindedly placed it on his finger.

Unfortunately, many hospitals are located in poor or nondescript neighborhoods. Such was the case at the Mercy Hospital. It was centered within a criminally active environment. The hospital security police patrolled, the area was well lit where possible, but still an occasional incident took place. Dino's thoughts were of going home. He reached his car, which was located in a dimly lit corner of the parking lot. As he was putting his key into the car door lock he felt a prodding into his ribs. A low voice whispered, "Give me your watch and your wallet."

Animal survival instincts took over. Dino spun around

and hit the hold-up man squarely in the jaw. Not realizing that his fist contained the heavy championship ring, he struck a knockout blow that sent the thug reeling to the pavement, stone cold out, the gun by his side.

Security Police were called. They assessed the situation, conferred amongst themselves and then told the doctor that he was crazy.

"Why did you risk your life for a few dollars?" they asked. Dino replied that he had never intended to resist the attacker, but his instincts had just taken over. He did add that he was pleased with the result!

"Get out of here, doc, before he wakes up. It will make things easier for all of us." Dino drove off with a glow of achievement as he looked back at the still prone thief lying on the parking lot pavement.

The next morning Dino looked over the chart of an individual who was admitted thorough the emergency room by the police the previous night. His jaw was fractured in several places and wired shut. Still, the wires would probably come off long before he was released from prison. The championship ring became a champion.

GENES III—The Legacy

The job was fulfilled. Dad's sage advice to "make the next generation better than yours" had been met. Dino's quartet of children grew up each forming a different branch on the strong trunk of the family tree. There was the artist, the musician, a model maker, philosopher, businessman and athlete, and even fireman or cowboy depending on the day and time of year. All have matured into responsible grownups that have followed their dreams. Not to slight the accomplishments of the other siblings in any way, for this story we will concentrate on Tony.

Antone J.Tatooles, MD, was supposed to be an engineer. He built model airplanes, cars, and boats at his workbench in the basement. A radio controlled helicopter was his pride and joy. Those early efforts culminated in a BS degree in Biomedical Engineering at Northwestern University. His biomedical interest triggered a career path deviation. With more years of schooling, Tony was able to earn a Medical Degree as well. When queried, "Why the change?" Tony reflected, "Growing up I observed my father's love for his work. Not only did Dad's enthusiasm for cardiac surgery entice me to pursue this career but also the fact that so many aspects of science are involved in the care of a patient with cardiac disease. It requires understanding medicine with an emphasis on anatomy, pathology and physiology. It requires exact surgical technique and efficiency to achieve great results." Dino was pleasantly surprised with Tony's choice.

Tony trained as an intern, resident and general surgeon at Northwestern University. Then the big step came when he elected to follow even further in his Dad's footsteps. He was accepted as a cardiothoracic surgical resident at the prestigious *Brigham and Women's Hospital* in Boston. Tony became a board certified cardiothoracic surgeon, just like Dad, but with a twist—his engineering background took him to another world in the advancement of patient care.

Tony was one of the first doctors to study and perform robotic surgery, a unique marriage of engineering and medicine. Such surgeons sit in a quiet corner of the operating room in front of a monitor controlling robotic mechanical arms located across the room above the operating table. These arms are two thousand times more sensitive than a human hand, and they can work all day and never tire. Micro controlled arms allow the surgeon to be more precise and to operate in smaller spaces than a hand would permit. Procedures that would previously have required the chest to be opened can now often be performed through small incisions.

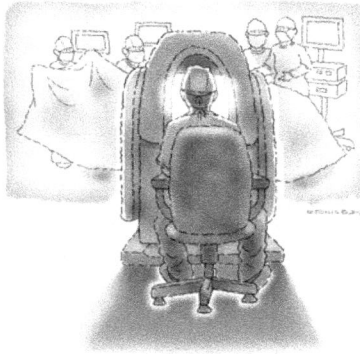

The majority of today's procedures, however, are still carried out totally hands on. Operations always require a competently trained doctor and support staff. The skilled hands of the surgeon cannot be replaced by machines. When asked where all this may lead to, Tony replied, "I believe physicians need to embrace new technology to advance medicine. Robots will not likely soon replace surgeons but new tools and a better understanding of biology will continue to make us better doctors. It is an exciting time to be involved in the progress of medicine."

In many cases organ replacement is still the only cure available. Kidneys were the first to be replaced after rejection drugs were perfected. A heart replacement was once unthinkable. When Drs. Norman Shumway and Christian Barnard first performed heart transplants, those operations were considered to be just short of "stunts". Today, even combined heart-lung transplants are being completed successfully.

Of course donor organ availability is a continuing problem. Patients frequently wait long periods of time for a suitable heart. Death was not infrequently the result of the wait. Now, heart pumps are hooked up to patients to keep them alive until a suitable heart donor can be found. Today's heart assist pumps, going back to Dr. Michael De Bakey's crude artificial heart later refined by Dr. Jarvic, are so reliable that some devices are implanted permanently, much like a heart pacemaker, and supplant the need of a donor heart. Using the newest technologies in the artificial heart field, Tony's group, at *Advocate Christ Medical Center* in suburban Chicago, performs transplants and installs implant assist devices routinely. Dr. Norman Shumway must be smiling as he watches from above.

The temper of the cardiovascular surgeon's life is still composed of long hours, unexpected calls and stressful periods of intense concentration. This was a recipe for disaster in the life of yesterday's sole practitioners. Today, Tony works as one of a highly skilled, well-trained and dedicated group of surgeons. Aside from some time for rest, this association also provides for constant critique, continual training and time for research. The combined best care is provided to the patient because of the insight and wisdom of the entire group.

Especially with today's task specialization, it is normal for all personnel to feel like equals, each doing his necessary part to ensure a successful outcome. Fortunately, everyone in the operating room is well trained, capable and knows their tasks. Like a winning football team, you need a great quarterback to win, but even the water boy is needed to quench the star's thirst. Their group functions like super bowl champs.

Tony reflected on status. "In my dad's day the heart surgeon was treated like a superstar or god. Nurses cringed at the possibility of making a mistake; staff did not speak to the surgeon unless he spoke to them first. All of the pioneer surgeons of Dad's generation that I have met were and are personable, passionate, great leaders and role models. However, I do agree that the days of the superstar are limited. Subsequent generations of surgeons will be more regulated with rigid rules and different expectations of results. Standardization is becoming the norm with most doctors now working with prescribed protocols.

"I also learned that my dad was not one of the

perceived conceited types. It is impressive how many physicians Dad had trained that today continue to speak so highly of him. They all loved and respected him because he treated everyone in a friendly and pleasant way." Again, Tony is a continuum of his dad: he is also respected and loved.

Like his dad, whenever he is at a social gathering, Tony is constantly being asked those same pesky medical questions that have followed physicians since the profession began. He always takes time to methodically listen and give an opinion or his advice. Although the answers may be technically different today, the questioner's objective still remains to "talk to an understanding doctor". In the meantime, he is also following our dad's sage advice; with the help of his wife, Laura, they are now preparing their kids to become the next better generation.

EPILOGUE

Goals remain the same, to improve the quality and extend the lives of people. Using modern equipment and innovative techniques, contemporary doctors are attaining outcomes unimagined by those early pioneers. Never to be forgotten however, today's achievements are a testament to the pioneers' belief that something better could be achieved. They continue to be an inspiration to those who will follow. To paraphrase an old quote, "You Ain't Seen Nothing yet."

The 2014 *American Heart Association Statistical Report* indicates just how far inpatient treatment of CVD, (Cardio-Vascular Diseases) has advanced. From 2000 to 2010 there was a 28% increase of cases (5,930,000 to 7,588,000). Continuing with that increase, today's results are certainly as impressive.

- Ages of 60-65 were considered upper limits of patient candidates.
- Today 80-85 year old patients are routinely accepted.
- Hospital stays have been reduced from an average of 5-10 days to 2-5 days.
- Patients that previously had no hope of survival now can have extended lives of 5-10 years.
- Many open heart operations have been replaced with non-invasive procedures.
- Mortality and morbidity rates have fallen to almost zero-tolerance levels.

Heart transplantation and artificial heart devices are the targets of biological research. The days of rebuilding rather than replacing may not be that far in the future. Exciting new advancements are anticipated from the next generation of doctors continuing in the spirit of those "innovative pioneers".

.

ACKNOWLEDGMENTS

$\mathcal{A}$cknowledgement pages remind me of thank you speeches at the Oscars. Thus, I must mention my sixth grade English teacher, Mrs. Foote, who was a stickler for grammar. Likewise, I cannot overlook my Uncle Pete who sat with me at the kitchen table to encourage my scribbling when I was a toddler. Where does irrelevance end?

Many people, however, have been directly responsible for this undertaking. First, of course, my brother Dino; without him there is no story. Throughout our lifetime we enjoyed many hours together relating experiences of our careers. His stories, however, had been more diverse than, and not as boring as, construction stories. One afternoon, while having a drink at the Wilmette golf course, we outlined some stories on a napkin. From an innocuous beginning, others later contributed their remembrances and helped to transform that napkin into this book.

Enlightened illustrations by Tom C. Katsulis set this project apart from just another memoir; his interpretive artwork captures ones imagination while reading the stories. The whimsical cover, rendered in "Hospital Blue" conveys the lighthearted nature of the book. It amazes me how perceptively the drawings relate to the medical world.

Manuscript drafts were reviewed by some of the doctors included in the book. I wish to thank Doctors Albert D. Pacifico, University of Alabama; Thomas J. Fogarty, Stanford University; Edward Diethrich, founder of the Arizona Heart Institute and Alex Doolas, retired Chief of Surgery at Rush University, Chicago, for their time, comments and encouragement. A special note of appreciation is given to Dr. Denton A. Cooley, President Emeritus of the Texas Heart Institute, for his Forward to the book. Mary Flannery, Dino's scrub nurse for over twenty years, was kind enough to add her personal observations.

The pioneers are recognized for their work to date. As a proud uncle, I was exposed to the latest techniques and the future direction of cardiovascular medicine by Dino's son, Anton J. "Tony" Tatooles, M.D. The saga is never-ending and getting better every day, bringing honor to those who forged the way.

My sincere thanks, also, to my cousins Elaine Markoutsas, writer, and husband Charles Le Roux, retired editor of the Chicago Tribune, for their critical review and suggestions. I appreciate the time that Nicholas Markos spent with us helping to formulate the transition of a manuscript into a book.

Back to relevance, I thank my wife Didi for putting up with my 2:00 am disturbances while I crawled out of bed to jot an idea or finish a section. Since we are fortunate to have a close-knit family, many others knowingly or unknowingly contributed to story recollections, and I thank all of them for their patience and understanding.

And finally, a special thanks to literary agent Nancy Brook Stavin, who was instrumental in bringing us to David Ross and Open Books.

If I have offended anyone in the course of this project, it surely was unintentional and I ask your understanding. Likewise, for those that contributed to the book and have been overlooked, again it was unintentional, and I ask your understanding as well.

James E. Tatooles
Estero, Florida

About James E. Tatooles

*J*ames E. Tatooles was born in Chicago in 1933 during the waning days of the depression. Together with his brother, "Dino", Jim was raised in a diverse ethnic neighborhood on the North side of Chicago.

He holds a BS in Mechanical Engineering from Rose-Hulman Institute of Technology, served a two year stint in the Army Corp of Engineers in Germany, and earned an MBA in the Kellogg School of Business at Northwestern University. After fifty years of building housing developments, commercial and industrial buildings throughout Chicago, Jim moved to Florida with Didi, his wife and backbone.

Uncle Pete sparked Jim's interest in writing at an early age, watching him scribble stories in a wide lined spiral notebook. Jim enjoys being a story teller and family history chronicler. But most of all, Jim is happiest when in the midst of his family and friends including his three children and six grandchildren.

About Constantine J. "Dino" Tatooles, MD

Constantine "Dino" Tatooles, M.D., the second son of John and Angela Tatooles, was born in Chicago, three years after his brother Jim, in May of 1936. Dino started his career at Budlong Grammar School, graduating as President of his class. At St. George High School in Evanston, he prepared for a medical career. Dino finished four years of pre-med studies at Albion College, Michigan, in three years. Dino attended the Strich School of Medicine at Loyola University of Chicago, where he received a Master's degree in Physiology along with his M.D. diploma, being the second person in the school history to receive two degrees at graduation.

His internship was at the University of Chicago. While there he was awarded the coveted Coller Clinical Tour scholarship. He then left U of C to train at the National Institute of Health's National Heart Institute, one of only five entrants accepted from a National Competition. After two years he was back at the U of C, specializing in Cardio-Thoracic Surgery. Next came a one year tour as a registrar in Pediatric Cardiac Surgery at the prestigious

Hospital for Sick Children on Great Ormond Street in London, England.

Dino returned to join the surgical staff at the Loyola University Hospital in Maywood, Illinois, where he performed the very first open heart procedure in the newly completed facility. He was later appointed the Chief of Surgery at the renowned Cook County Hospital of Chicago. During his 10 years there he also taught at the University of Illinois Medical School and Hospital where he became their youngest full professor. Dino continued to be on the staff and lecture at Illinois, after he left Cook County to start a private practice at St. Francis Hospital in Evanston, Illinois; he remained there for the next twenty five years.

Interspersed with the private practice, Dino traveled extensively. As a member of the International College of Surgeons, Dino operated or lectured on Pediatric Surgery in Bergamo, Italy; London, England; Athens, Greece; Bordeaux, France, and the Monti Carlo Vascular Institute. Throughout the course of his career he was a presenter or speaker at many meetings throughout the states as well. Coupled with the above, he has received countless awards and recognition for his work and research.

Dino has been blessed with a wonderful supporting family; Betty, his wife of over fifty years, four children and ten great grandkids.

About Thomas C. Katsulis

After graduating from Bradley University, Tom gained experience on the creative staffs of several select Chicago ad agencies. Preferring the challenge and creativity of working on a variety of accounts, Tom chose to become a freelance illustrator and worked on projects for such agencies as Leo Burnett, J. Walter Thompson, DraftFCB, and others. Some of the well-known accounts to which Tom has contributed include Keebler, Raid, Scrubbing Bubbles, Cap'n Crunch, McDonald's and Disney.

www.ingramcontent.com/pod-product-compliance
Lightning Source LLC
Chambersburg PA
CBHW072127090426
42739CB00012B/3093